Starting
as a
student

A Christian approach

David Jackman

Inter-Varsity Press

© INTER-VARSITY PRESS, LONDON

Universities and Colleges Christian Fellowship
39 Bedford Square
London WC1B 3EY

ISBN 0 85110 374 x

First published May 1974
Reprinted August 1974

Printed in Great Britain by
Wright's (Sandbach) Ltd., Sandbach, Cheshire

Starting as a student

Contents

Acknowledgments

The material in this book is derived largely from six years' work among Christian Unions in the universities of Britain. The author gratefully acknowledges the ideas and help of many colleagues on the staff of the Universities and Colleges Christian Fellowship, and of Christian Union student leaders. He is particularly grateful to Michael Wenham, whose helpful comments and suggestions on reading the initial manuscript have added greatly to its scope, and to Miss Christine King for her typing.

He is also indebted to Oliver Barclay's *The Christian's Approach to University Life* and Myre Sim's *Tutors and their Students* for some outline ideas and much stimulus to thought.

1 Entering orbit

So, at last, you've made it! After all the work at 'A' levels, all the form-filling and applications, college life is starting.

Entering a new orbit isn't an everyday experience, which makes it all the more stimulating, but also involves all sorts of adjustments. Many of them take place quite normally and painlessly, of course, and no-one needs a book to help him make them. So why this one?

Don't think that this is aiming to squeeze you into a stereotyped mould, or to give you six easy lessons on how to become the all-purpose, successful student! College situations vary enormously, as do the people in them. All of us react differently because we are individuals and have a God-given personality that is unique. It is our personal choices in a host of different circumstances which combine to make us mature people. What this book is designed to do is to provide some data and suggestions in those areas of student life where it can be of real value to know a little about what to expect. It could help you to think through more adequately the choices that will shape your life, so that your God-given individuality can be more fully developed.

Being a Christian makes fundamental differences to every area of life. We have a new Lord to serve, a new power with which to do this, new goals for which to live. We want to know Christ better, love him more and serve him more faithfully. So the Christian looks at his student days, as he does at all the rest of his life, quite differently from the viewpoint of his friends who are not yet Christians. But he is no less a student than they are, and he will share many of the experiences, frustrations and excitements common to student life generally. As a

Christian student he can't help being different, not in a self-conscious way but by virtue of his beliefs, standards, behaviour, values. He wouldn't want to avoid it. This isn't a barrier to cut him off from others so much as a distinctive way of life which marks him out. As a Christian *student*, however, he also finds that his life is very different from that of many of his fellow-Christians, in his church, for example. Again, it is easy for this to become a barrier that separates, so that he can imagine he really is different just because he happens to be at college.

It is important to realize that such external differences matter very little. The Christian student is still first and foremost a Christian, who has the same basic needs, faces the same temptations, experiences the same battles and draws on the same resources as the whole family of God. He has been set free by Christ to be the unique personality God has designed him to be — to be himself — and for a few years that privilege is going to be enjoyed in the exciting and challenging whirlpool of life as a student.

Freedom at last!

Perhaps the greatest characteristic of this new area of life is its freedom. Life is no longer governed by school rules and school bells. You can lie in bed rather than go to lectures if you want to. You don't have to stay in the library if the sun is shining. You choose what you wear, what you eat, where you live, whom you get to know. You set your own pace and style of living. There is less direct pressure on you to make you work. After all, you are at college because you have chosen to be there.

Most of us would put personal freedom very high on our list of things worth fighting for, and yet freedom in itself is a neutral thing. It has to be used. It is in the using of it that the character of the free man is gradually shaped and increasingly demonstrated. But any freedom, to be exercised and enjoyed, depends upon an ordered structure of some sort. Every society has its rules and accepted codes, simply because, if everyone were entirely 'free', the resulting anarchy would mean that no-one was really free at all. The Highway Code isn't designed to take the thrill out of motoring so much as to ensure that you are free to enjoy your mobility in comparative safety. The Christian recognizes in the same way that the personal freedom God has given him can be fulfilled only by being exercised within God's given structures. He realizes that God is the author of order out of chaos and that God's character is expressed in the structures which he has given to human relationships in society, within which we can act and choose with real freedom and significance.

This will apply especially to the community of the college or university for the Christian who is starting as a student. It does not mean that the Christian is always by definition an 'establishment' man, that he accepts uncritically every structure with which he is presented and mildly accedes to it, however restrictive or unjust it is. He will want to make a clear distinction between what is God-given and what is man-made in the laws governing the society in which he lives. Believing that there are certain principles which God has revealed for the benefit of man, he will be most concerned to see these operating in his community, not because he wants to impose Christian values on a non-Christian world, but because he is convinced that they provide the only reliable foundation on which to operate. They are true to man, as he is — as God made him. If particular, man-made structures need to be reformed, Christians should play a leading part in seeking to bring them as near the God-given norms for human life as they can. We want to use our freedom to function as the Maker intended.

Sorting things out

So one of the most exciting areas of experience facing the new student who is a Christian is working out how the Bible's teaching is to apply in practice to the whole of his life and the community where God has placed him. Of course this is the task of a lifetime! One of the joys of growing as a Christian is finding how biblical truth impinges on more and more areas of one's life and thought. I am not suggesting that you sit down and solemnly work out a complete Christian 'system' during your first term at college or university. We don't usually come at these things cold; they tend to be hammered out in the thick of life's pressures. But as Christians we do have in the Bible our base of revealed truth from which to work and on which to build as we cope with the complexities of living in our new environment. It will need working at because most of us tend to accept fairly uncritically, while at home in a circle of friends we know well, the traditions in which we have grown up. We fit in; and a good deal of our behaviour is conditioned by what is generally acceptable in the group.

This can be particularly the case with regard to our Christian experience and attitudes. It is quite possible to come up to college from a Christian family, or from a church or youth group, without ever having worked out for yourself *why* you do or do not believe certain things, or why you live the way you do. Life at college soon brings heavy pressure on you to sort things out. Some Christians discover that, although they have a personal faith, they have relied too much on their home group or fellowship to carry them along and do their thinking for them. It's easy to accept traditions and assimilate teaching without ever thinking it through for yourself, or even questioning its validity. Others discover that much of their faith is second-hand too. It may have been easy to drift with the crowd in a Christian environment at home, but at college, where anti-Christian pressures are considerable, drifting won't preserve your Christianity. You need the strength of a personal relationship with Christ to swim against the tide.

It pays to do some thinking. This is one of the main aims of further education anyway, and we mustn't be afraid of subjecting our beliefs to a rigorous examination. Often the impetus comes from friends who are not yet Christians themselves. Why *are* you a Christian? What difference do you reckon it makes in your life? Why do you believe the Bible? What's this 'personal relationship' with Christ? How did you get it? How can you be so sure? The first few weeks of student life are often crucial in facing up to questions like these. They provide great opportunities if we have answers or are prepared to do some hard thinking to find them. Sadly, Christians are too often caught mumbling some half-remembered cliché which does not even convince them.

This doesn't mean, of course, that we aim to become a sort of 'ideal' Christian student, rather like a religious slot-machine, which produces 'right' answers (complete with text) neatly packaged, when fed with an appropriate question. Nor does the Christian imagine he has got everything sewn up, if he has an ounce of humility, or sense! There is always more truth to be discovered in the Bible and further areas of life to which it must be applied at greater depth.

Some of the questions to be faced are vast and quite unanswerable in any pat, pre-digested form: Why does a God of love permit so much suffering in the world? What happens to those who have never heard of Christ? How do you know that Christianity is the *only* way to God? Is 'religion' anything more than a psychological prop?[1] These, and many others, are problems that we must grapple with, if we are to be honest. We have absolutely nothing to lose. Indeed, Christian faith, committed as it is to the Christ who is truth, can only be strengthened by this sort of honest enquiry. It does underline the importance, however, of gaining a working knowledge of the Bible's teaching, some awareness of how it all fits together and its application to daily living. This must be a priority for the Christian at college.

[1] For a start towards answering these and other questions, see Paul Little's book *How To Give Away Your Faith* (IVP).

The great characteristic of the Christian student is that he is committed to truth. His personal life is grounded in a living relationship with the living God, in and through the Lord Jesus Christ. This provides him not only with true principles on which to build, but a person of strength and truth to know and worship, love and serve. His whole life, including his study, is a penetration into God's world. He will not necessarily be the most accurate observer, or gifted analyst, but he will be operating in a context of reality, because he has found the God who is truth, or rather been found by him.

All students organize their lives and work according to some set of beliefs or presuppositions (however cynical) which colour their judgments and dictate their values. The Christian has no need to be ashamed of his beliefs. He must learn to argue them and defend them, most of all to live them with sincerity, because he knows that his life-style, his priorities, his choices and his future depend upon the divine revelation of unchanging truth.

2 Those first few days

They may even be so glad to see you that they put on a welcoming party at the railway station. With many halls and digs being way out of town, a lot of colleges lay on a shuttle service to welcome their new students and get them to their rooms. Or you may prefer to drive into town anonymously and begin to find your own way around. Either way you will soon discover that everybody around the place seems to be geared up to one major aim — to welcome (and preferably sign up) *you* — the new student. The word 'fresher' seems a bit out of fashion these days. But whatever they call you, they certainly seem to be glad to see you and the student world seems an incredibly friendly place.

Assuming, then, that you have reached your destination and found that the room really is meant for you, you are now in residence. Where you live will be one of the biggest factors in your process of adjustment to student life, and it is of course impossible to generalize. Most people find that it helps to live in a hall of residence during the first year if they can. You are able to get to know a wide range of people this way. Everything is 'on tap' and readily accessible; you don't have to worry about shopping and cooking. But it's never disastrous if there's no room in hall for you, and some people do so well in the digs they get in the first year that they stay put for the rest of their course.

Adjustment also depends to quite a considerable extent on the sort of institution you find yourself a member of. It may be a collegiate university where the residential college provides the main living unit and where it is possible to get to know virtually everybody.

On the other hand some of the larger polytechnics and civic universities have such enormous accommodation problems that digs or flats may be situated many miles out from the campus, and you will find yourself cast in the rôle of commuter, travelling in and out on a nine-to-five work shift. This is especially the case if your digs provide bed, breakfast and evening meal. Increasingly it seems that people will be forced to live at home as the number of students continues to rise and accommodation cannot keep pace. Digs can have their compensations, in that they are usually cheaper, and if you have a good landlady you may find yourself fitting into a much more normal family community than hall provides.

Wherever you are and whatever the pattern of life there, reckon that if it is really bad you can always change, and be prepared to adapt as much as you can to the realities of the situation. In severe cases, find the college lodgings officer and see if you can get help in discovering something more suitable. Go where students meet and you won't feel like a fish out of water for very long.

Making friends

One of the most encouraging things to remember as you begin college life is that almost everyone else will be as lonely as you are and equally wanting to make friends. In this situation there is nothing to stop you from taking the initiative, and you may well find it very rewarding. Hopefully your trunk has arrived, so all you need to do is find your supply of mugs and spoons, get some instant coffee and plastic milk, and you're ready to meet your new friends.

The best way to make friends is to be friendly. So often the student who complains of loneliness has only himself to blame. There are other people across the corridor who would be only too pleased to accept an invitation to get to know one another. If you live a long way out in digs and feel remote and cut off, remember you can get to know the people who are next to you in lectures, in the

14

lab or canteen, or on the train or bus going out to your part of the city. They sit next to you in the library or launderette. There is no need to be alone any more than you choose to be. Be typically un-British! Spend the first couple of weeks asking everyone you meet their name and it's surprising how many people you will get to know! But at the same time make sure that you are making some deeper and definite friendships with a few particular people, both Christians and non-Christians. It is possible to know lots of people superficially and yet be the genuine friend of none. You may be surprised how quickly groups of friends bind together, how soon the cliques jell. After a few weeks it can be quite hard to break into them.

If you are a Christian you will want your life, already given to God, to count for him while you are at college and to benefit others. God wants us not to live for ourselves, but to share all that we have, including our own selves (1 Thes. 2:8), with others. The Christian life is one of giving ourselves away. Anything we have — talents, time, possessions — is a gift from God, and so it is not ours to keep and hoard, but to use in giving.

It is worth while thinking this out with reference to certain specifics. What about your room? You tend to think of it as yours. Many people, when they involuntarily have to share with a room-mate, even divide the room into his or hers and mine, so as to keep their territory inviolate. That's not a good way to build a friendship. And if you have a single room, are you willing for others to use it, to drop in as if it were their own? What about your work? If you are pretty good at your subject and there's another student in your group who is having a terrible job squeezing through, don't just pray for him. Set aside some time each week to help him. What about money? If a girl is having a tough time making ends meet, don't buy your new outfit and pray for her. Give her some practical help.

To share yourself like this may mean showing real friendship to someone who does not reciprocate. It may

15

mean a friendship with someone who is really hard to befriend and whom other people tend to avoid. It may involve giving up what you want to do all the time and following somebody else's line. But isn't this what Jesus meant when he talked about denying ourselves? He commanded it. And in giving like this you will also find that you receive, and that you are changing. You won't just dissociate yourself from the studious bookworm, but you'll learn from him. You won't be so critical of the girl who takes trouble with her appearance, but will spend a little more time on your own. Many students could, with great profit! There is no need to look like a refugee. Similarly the person who can't afford to be better dressed is not to be despised, but valued for his honesty and friendliness. There are so many ways in which we can help other people and find our own lives immeasurably enriched as a result.

Your grant

Official information, of varying degrees of importance, will bombard you from your arrival, throughout your entire first term. Tutors, clubs, societies, Students Union, mass radiography and every life insurance company you ever heard of compete greedily for your time and interest. Try to sort out the really important ones, such as interviews with tutors, but don't be too overawed by the mountain of material.

Among this welter of information will come the cheerful news that your grant is available for collection. It will hardly be a princely sum, but most people manage. The emphasis, though, is definitely on management. If you haven't opened a bank account, the major (and minor) banks are ready to compete for your custom and will be advertising widely. Most students find it very hard to predict how long their grant will last and it's certainly not a bad idea to err on the side of caution for the first few weeks. The hi-fi can wait until you see how the essentials of student life — meals, books, travel, coffee —

work out. Most department stores, however, tend to be cleaned out of black socks and shirts (you don't have to wash them!) within ten days of the start of term. But it would be a pity to be sartorially elegant and starve, so do make sure you have enough to buy adequate food and, if you are self-catering (especially if you are a girl with ideas on slimming), that you do get one square meal a day. You cannot possibly exist on sausage and chips for ever, not even with occasional baked beans, so it's only sense from the point of view of doing your work adequately to make financial provision for a proper diet.

It's also a good idea at the beginning not to buy every book that is recommended to you. Most students probably spend too little on books, being prepared to suffer the frustrations of waiting for the one library copy to go round so that they can spend their money on other things. But part of your grant is intended for books and there will be some which are really indispensable tools for your course work, reference books which you will need in your professional career when college days are over. Buy them; but remember that you may well be able to get them cheaply second-hand in a Union sale a little later on in term. It's a good idea to ask someone in the second or third year of your course which books are essential, and then shop around a bit for a suitable second-hand copy, though beware of cheap editions which may be out of date.

Finding time

Within the first week you will probably be introduced to your department or faculty, start to find your way around the campus, and generally settle in. If you live in hall you may be treated to a procession of representatives of every conceivable club and society, eager to enlist your support for the year ahead. This usually culminates in the Freshers' Bazaar or Societies' Fair in which each of these societies mans a stall, all under the same roof, and endeavours to out-shout and out-bid all the others in its

17

efforts to secure your subscription, without which it may not survive. It's all great fun, especially if you resolve not to part with any money on the spot, and don't actually join more than two or three groups. If you do, it will just be a waste of money, since no-one can in practice be an active member of more than that number of clubs — and still remain a student!

Do make up your mind to join some clubs and societies, though, as they are a good way of getting to know a cross-section of people and have real value in their own right. You may like to tackle some pastime that is entirely new, or play your favourite sport regularly, possibly for a team, or get involved in Union affairs, in the student newspaper or campus radio and television. There's no shortage of things to do and now is the time to explore anything that you are remotely interested in.

But the commodity that is in shortest supply in student life is time. You probably have about 750 days in which to make your student career, and in many places it is a good deal shorter than that. So you will need to make the most of the time and it is the easiest thing in the world to kill it, waste it or fritter it away. The whole secret is to get a good balance of activities, and that requires experiment, trial and error, and discipline. A great deal of your enjoyment of student life hinges upon having a sensible, workable daily pattern.

One student described his experience in leaving home to go to college in terms of a dog who had been chained in the back yard all his life. Suddenly the chain was broken. He could do anything he wanted from now on. And that's how he spent his first year, doing everything that had been forbidden before. A Christian student wrote from his university: 'I came here expecting to turn this place upside down for the Lord. Instead, this place has almost turned me upside down for the devil.' So the question is how to use your freedom in the right way.

Try, then, to get into some sort of pattern during the first few days, not a rut from which you never move, but a flexible structure which enables you to experiment and develop all the different aspects of your student life. Everybody will have a different set of priorities and we each have to work out our own. Our academic work must feature very high on that list and we must do all we can to establish a pattern from the beginning in which it is adequately covered. For example, it seems to be a general rule that time lost in the morning is never regained during the day. It's probably a danger sign if breakfast is becoming something of a non-event in your schedule. You may not eat it, but you ought to have surfaced by that time! Conversations that have a brilliant sparkle at 1 a.m. look rather less brilliant in the cold light of dawn. It's great fun and can be very stimulating to talk and argue late into the night, but it is probably a good idea not to allow yourself the luxury too often.

If you are a Christian, the perspective in which you look at all these things will be that of God's control and guidance in your life. This means relaxation rather than tension, and peace instead of anxiety, because you are living a day at a time under his direction. This episode in your life is part of his wise plan, as he develops your talents and personality in bringing you to maturity in Christ. The Bible metaphor of the 'steward' is important here. Entrusted with his master's resources, his chief requirement is faithfulness, reliability. If we are prepared to give all we can and be our best for God and for others, we shall not go far wrong.

The folks at home

It's very easy to be so swamped by all the activities that you forget the folks at home, but do try to 'phone or write to parents and family regularly; they do like to keep in touch. The Christian student will also want to keep the church, and especially his friends in the young people's group, well informed of how things are developing. They may well write to you, send you the church newsletter or parish magazine and other literature describing any

19

special activities that are going on at home. Some groups arrange a circular letter about half-way through term giving plenty of news about people and situations, and if it is useless to pretend that you will ever be a regular letter-writer, you may at least be able to send in a paragraph or two for that. Do everything you can to keep the links strong. The vacation will soon come round and you will need this continuing fellowship. The more you feed your friends at home with information for praise and prayer, the more they will keep you in touch and the stronger will be the mutual support and encouragement you can give.

Do give a bit of thought also during term as to how you are going to invest your vacations. You may need to spend most of the time working, either academically or for financial reasons, but many students could give a week or two to help in their home church with visitation, evangelism, or decorating the premises. There are many contributions that can be made if you have a mind for them and are prepared not to drift away from your old environment simply because for half the year you are in a different one.

God is real

So as you begin to settle in and enjoy student life, try to keep yourself and what you are doing in perspective. Much of what you have already discovered about being a disciple of Christ will be left unsaid in this book. But, however you react to your new environment, remember that the same means of grace are open to you; the same principles for living the Christian life apply; the same temptations occur; the same Lord is rich to all who call on him. What we become as people, our usefulness or otherwise in the world, as well as the success of our student career, depends very much upon how far we make the Lord Jesus Christ central in all we do.

I remember being challenged, as a student, by a speaker to our Christian Union who asked what difference it would have made to our living that day if Christ had not really been alive. Any difference at all, or had we been living out of direct contact with him? This is the acid test of any Christian life or profession. If Paul's great ambition was to know him (Phil. 3:8, 10) and to please him, ours can be no less.

Perhaps as you read this chapter you feel that much of it is rather strange and remote from you because you have not yet recognized that Jesus Christ really is the Lord. Thousands of students have come into a living relationship with God at the very beginning of their student careers by honestly facing up to the claims of Christ and finding them to be true, and Jesus to be real. They have discovered in Jesus Christ God's demonstration, in terms that we can understand (a human life), of his own nature and character. They have realized that the historical Jesus, who lived a life of perfection, has set for all time the standard by which mankind is to be judged, and they have seen the shabbiness and sin of their own lives when placed alongside God's proper man. But they have also recognized in that atoning death on the cross God's provision for mankind, alienated as we are by sin and selfishness, lost and dead to God. For the God-man, Jesus Christ, who lived the life that we have failed to live, died the death that we deserve to die. The way to God is open. There is forgiveness for sin, removal of guilt and new life for all those who, turning from their sin, believe in Christ and commit their lives into God's hands. This is the start of true Christian experience, the beginning of eternal life, and without it we cannot even attempt to live as Christians, at college or anywhere else. All that this book covers in experience is impossible unless God is alive and living in the individual Christian to give his love, joy and strength for our need.

This then is the constant reality of Christian experience. God is real. He does guide and direct, equip and strengthen, because he lives within the personality that is given over to him. The genius of the gospel is that God

21

is at work in us, even when we feel totally incompetent, giving us the ability to live in a way that honours and pleases him, and helps others. The Christian life is not a matter of following a list of precepts, but its beginning and end are in Christ, in a personal living relationship with him each day. He is our motivation. He is our message. This can be your experience too. For the Christian, who knows the truth of these things in his life, there is the continuing imperative of Christ, wherever we are, to seek first his kingdom and righteousness knowing that all we need will then be added to us (Mt. 6:33).

God is no man's debtor. No man ever put the values of Christ first and lost out. So let us be whole-hearted and disciplined in our Christian living. We are called to be learners (disciples), not mere camp-followers. Let us resolve at the very beginning of life as a student that, by God's grace, we will not fall prey to mental pride or to intellectual snobbery, that we will not allow the world to squeeze us into its mould, or to seal our lips, but that, as disciples, we shall make disciples, until in the student world it is known that there is a God in heaven, that Jesus Christ is the living Lord and Saviour, and that 'these men who have turned the world upside down have come here also'.

3 Academic work

'I really ought to go and do some work' must be one of the most common sentences in student life. You can hear it any night of the week, as another cup of coffee is poured, in a thousand student residences. But it highlights one of the crucial areas of adjustment for the new student, and the annual wastage rate, either through failing exams or dropping out from courses, illustrates that there are some students who never really come to grips with it at all.

Most students find that there are considerable differences between school and college learning situations. Increasingly schools are adopting college methods in their 'A' level courses, with personal tuition and seminars playing an important part, which helps to make the transition easier. But there are still definite contrasts. At school the structures are fairly rigid and the pressure to succeed comes from home, or from the staff, or from competition with other people you know well. But in student life there are few direct pressures of this sort. It is often up to the individual to decide how much time to spend on his work, how far to follow up new ideas, which lectures to attend. Tutors seem more remote and, while they are approachable enough, they are often occupied with their own research, or there is an appointments system which means that informal contacts are rare. There isn't the personal attention which a small sixth form provides. Now you are one unit in a course group of perhaps hundreds, and it is easy to believe (at the beginning anyway!) that they are all getting on better with the subject than you are. Many students suddenly realize how well they were 'crammed' at school and how little real exploring or thinking in their subjects they have done for themselves. Several have told me how overwhelmed they were by the first term in which all their ideas were systematically demolished, so that they were forced to build from scratch. These are common problems and no-one should consider them to be unique.

Perhaps the most important change to grasp is that in college life you really have to make the running yourself. The impetus to work comes from your own interest and enthusiasm, rather than from external pressures. So it is helpful to settle firmly in your thinking that work is one of the major ingredients of student life and to make up your mind to do your best in this area as consistently as you possibly can. For the Christian this is an important resolve, because it is fatally easy to see academic work as an unfortunately necessary interlude between bouts of really important 'spiritual' activity, such as evangelism, Christian meetings or social work. This is to misunderstand completely what being a student is all about. Going to college is a matter of personal choice; but it is a choice which implies certain responsibilities.

Significance of work

What, then, is the importance, or significance, of our academic work? Many of our difficulties in this area stem from the way in which we separate 'work' from the rest of our life, as though it was a special compartment. There is sometimes a tendency to regard ourselves as a warring mixture of body, mind and spirit, rather than as whole human beings. It has become fashionable to 'downgrade' the activities of the intellect, under the view that the mind of man is fallen and totally corrupt. The only meaningful level on which man can operate is the spiritual, by the activity of the Holy Spirit in the Christian. So, it is hinted, academic work is very much a second-rate activity for the Christian and some even go so far as to make 'commitment' or discipleship dependent upon renouncing all study except that of the Bible, leaving college and witnessing through a Christian commune.

24

I once met a most sincere Christian, who had been counselling a student facing considerable intellectual problems. The advice he had given was that, as the Lord warned his disciples to cut off the hand or to pluck out the eye if these were the cause of offence, in this case the only way was to 'cut off the head' and stop thinking! But why then has God given us minds? When we speak of man being created in the 'image' of God (Gn. 1:26) we are not thinking only of his original knowledge and righteousness which were lost by sin. There are also elements in the nature of man as man, such as intellectual abilities and moral freedom, which, although tainted by sin, still remain in man in spite of the Fall. Indeed, if man's rational or moral nature had been lost by the Fall, he would have no longer been man at all. It is his ability to think, as well as to choose, which marks him out from the rest of the creation. Consequently man is charged with the responsibility to 'fill the earth and subdue it; and have dominion' over the rest of the created order (Gn. 1:28).

Much of the record of human history is the story of fallen man attempting to fulfil his humanity in these respects, without reference to the God who created him, or obedience to his principles and commands. The Christian must at all costs not deny his humanity. God has given us minds with which to honour him; they are to be stretched and developed to the full. The words of Psalm 111:2 which are inscribed over the Cavendish Laboratory in Cambridge remain a thrilling reminder of our charter. 'Great are the works of the Lord, studied by all who have pleasure in them.'

Conflicts

The new student can, however, be shaken by the conflicts he meets at this very point. What of the lecture course which begins by attacking the Christian principles on which one's life is built? What of the theories and systems, particularly in the arts and social sciences, which are built on the assumption (not argued) that man is nothing but an animal or a machine, and which require almost as a basis for discussion the atheist assumption that God does not exist? The academic environment can be extremely hostile to Christian belief and the whole intellectual atmosphere can be destructive of personal faith. But this is drastic only where the Christian is unprepared for the battle, or unwilling to work and think things through.

It is important to remember that lecturers are not infallible. Academic competence in one discipline does not always confer wisdom in other areas of life. I have sometimes heard students arguing that if a certain lecturer says that no intelligent person (note the implication!) can believe the Bible to be anything more than a collection of cultic myths, then, because he is an expert on epic poetry, he must be right! It is of course entirely right that we should respect our intellectual superiors for their knowledge and experience, but this does not make their spiritual judgment automatically reliable.

The crucial point is to recognize that the lecturer is working from certain presuppositions, and in order to answer the case adequately we must discover what they are and how far they are justified. This is no easy task and we shall need a good deal of hard work and study to make progress. But even though we do not have all the answers to hand, it can be a great help to know *why* conclusions have been reached which seem so alien to the Christian understanding of life and the world. If we can see on what assumptions the case has been built, we shall have the beginnings of an answer. Not every student will feel intellectually capable of working out individual answers to academic challenges, but we can discuss it with other Christians in the same subject and keep up with the growing Christian literature in this area. There is real value in being driven back to examine our own presuppositions, and some colleges deliberately break down the preconceived ideas of their new intake, in order to force them back to basics and to work out a philosophy of life from scratch. This would be of even greater benefit if the vacuum were not so often filled by the most readily accessible alternative — the staff's own views!

If we can 'defuse' the situation from some of its emotional pressures, we shall probably be able to cope with it much better. For example, the whole realm of the miraculous and supernatural may be under fire, on the grounds that because miracles cannot happen in a mechanistic universe, they do not happen. The Christian student sees this as a threat to his or her own conversion experience, as well as to the authenticity of the Gospels, and is often paralysed from answering the problem on the basic presuppositional level, because of the in-built personal involvement and tension. Similar factors apply in the range of arguments which see religion as an opiate, or a psychological prop for those unable to cope with reality. Once we have filtered off the heavy emotional implications for ourselves, we shall be better able to deal with the assertion by means of the objective historical foundations of the Christian's faith.[1] If it is indeed the revealed truth of God, then the Christian faith has nothing to fear from such attacks. And if it is not, the sooner it is exposed the better.

We need never be afraid of thinking through our problems. There are far graver dangers inherent in refusing to think. Christianity has been under attack for the past 2,000 years and it is unlikely in the extreme that anyone is going to develop a new torpedo now. Indeed, attacks of this sort serve only to strengthen the truth, as new evidence is produced for its veracity. We are not to become 'slaves of men' (1 Cor. 7:23) by yielding to the prevailing climate of thought or by refusing to meet the challenges that will come to our faith.

Often the tension is greatest when we fail to hold on to the facts of faith, and concentrate on the experience of

[1] For further help in this area see J. N. D. Anderson, *Christianity: the Witness of History* (Tyndale Press).

27

feelings. We know that Christianity won't sink without us, but we shall sink without it. It's my own personal faith that is threatened. When this happens, we must return to the things we *do* know, however basic they may be. Go back to the person of Jesus of Nazareth, to the authenticity of the Gospels as historical records, to the cross and resurrection. While concentrating on the objective truths of Christianity, keep the subjective experience of God's presence warm and living. Tell him all about the problems, however overwhelming they may be. Ask for new light and heavenly wisdom. Read your Bible thoughtfully. Keep in touch with other Christians with whom you can talk and pray through the problems. Don't forget that doubts can be doubted too!

One great help in situations like this can be the existence of informal discussion groups for Christians studying similar academic subjects. These have sprung up spontaneously in a number of colleges and have given not only the opportunity of sharing common problems, but the encouragement and stimulus of thinking a way through them together. This is Christian fellowship in action, and if such a group does not exist in your department it may well be worth while forming one. But make sure its aim is solid biblical thinking, not just mutual commiseration. A second-hand faith will not last long in today's intellectual battles. We must make our faith our own, firmly grounding all our thinking in God's truth, and working at its application on every level of our living. Only then shall we really be able to love God with all our mind, and develop into the unique whole person he designed each of us to be.

Our first academic responsibility is therefore to God. We are not slaves, in the sense of those to whom Paul wrote, but his words are of lasting application. 'Whatever your task, work heartily, as serving the Lord and not men' (Col. 3:23). Similarly, to those who advocated dropping out of society in view of the imminence of the

Lord's return, he writes, 'If any one will not work, let him not eat. For we hear that some of you are living in idleness, mere busybodies, not doing any work. Now such persons we command and exhort in the Lord Jesus Christ to do their work in quietness and to earn their own living' (2 Thes. 3:10-12). As students our living, in term-time anyway, is provided by the state and/or our parents. Under God, we have a responsibility to them to do our work thoroughly.

Home backgrounds vary enormously. In some cases, parents may have serious misgivings about their children being at college at all, feeling that they should be 'doing a useful job of work'. In others, the successful academic career of their children seems to be an important factor in the parents' social status. For some, breaking away from home may cause a few tensions, but time will heal these. Mark Twain is reported as saying that when he was seventeen he thought his father knew nothing, but it was surprising what the old man had learnt by the time his son was twenty-one! As part of our 'honouring' our parents we shall keep them fully informed of what is happening and ask their advice wherever possible. Also there is a responsibility to our college or university. Having taken up a place for which there was probably considerable competition, we expect to take advantage of their facilities and teaching. In return they have a right to expect a serious contribution from their students.

Quality and quantity

We now turn to some of the more practical issues affecting our academic work. Everyone is agreed that a first-class result is not automatically guaranteed by working longer hours than anyone else. It is not the quantity so much as the quality of work that matters, and here concentration is the key factor. It's easy to look down a page without reading it, or to copy out words without mastering facts and arguments. We all have different patterns, partly formed by habit, and it is important to discover one's own optimum period of concentration. Some people work better if they take a short break after an hour, or change subjects every hour. Others prefer a stretch of several hours at one thing. We have to discover our personal preferences by experiment and not be unduly influenced by other people.

Part of the secret of good work is finding a congenial setting. If you cannot work against a background of noise, record players and interruptions, then your room in hall may not be the best place to attempt serious study. On the other hand, if you do your best work to a background of Radio One and half-hourly cups of coffee, it may be the only place you can function! Libraries are heaven to some and prison to others. Most students soon find their own best work times and places, but if you find you are having real problems of concentration, do discuss them with your tutor as soon as you can. Most courses are so structured that you cannot afford to drop badly behind.

What we can be sure of is that we all work better given regular breaks for relaxation and rest. The principle of one day off in seven is as old as creation, and is written by God into the structures of human life. Human beings are not made to function without the day of rest. Attempts within our own country to ride roughshod over this fact have all failed and while we hardly need research results to corroborate creation ordinances, it's interesting to see how the two agree. One university department of sociology recently attempted to correlate hours worked by students with their exam results. They discovered that those who regularly had one day a week completely free from academic work did consistently better than those who did not. The interesting feature is that those who had two days off often did better than both the others. Where this process stops may be open to some doubt! However, it does seem sensible for the Christian student to keep Sunday as a completely different day and to use it for worship and rest. The rest part is important too, because so often Christian students can make Sunday the most hectic day of the week, as they gallop from one meeting to another, with questionable value. A good way of making sure of the change, as well as rest, is to spend part of Sunday in the worship of a local church, where the college or university scene can be left behind. Similarly during the week it's good to have a range of activities so that it is not all work and no play.

Courses vary considerably in the amount of set work they demand, though most students work between a thirty- and forty-hour week including lectures, labs, tutorials and seminars. You will soon get the feel of your course and be able to identify the times when the work begins to pile up. It is obviously sensible to put in the extra hours as the work arrives if you can, rather than allow a backlog to develop so that you are never up to date. But even the best laid plans are liable to be swamped by a 'work crisis', when you just have to slog through until the assignment is completed. It can be quite fun, so long as it does not occur too frequently and provided that one doesn't become trapped in a vicious circle of late nights, poor sleep, late mornings, poor concentration.

One of the most rewarding and exciting features of college life is that the work can be so enjoyable. Sometimes when we complain about the dullness of our courses, it is because we do practically nothing ourselves to develop our own interest or enthusiasm for the subject. There will be periods of uninspiring routine, particularly in mastering the elements of a new subject or at the start of a course, but the same is true of any job. Many courses do provide opportunities for students to follow up aspects of the subject which are only briefly touched on in the syllabus and this can open all sorts of new avenues of thought and interest. To do only the 'set work' often means missing a really stimulating experience of puzzling something out for oneself which can inject new zest for work in a period of dull routine.

It is also helpful to work out, for example, what a lecture (which may be boring) is designed to do. Perhaps you can pick up from it a general outline of the scope and content of a particular subject which can be studied in detail later. Often a new thesis or line of thought will be raised which can trigger off new ideas for you to chase up. Try to see if you can get something positive out of it! But of course there is ultimately little value in sitting loyally through a series of irrelevant or incomprehensible lectures or, worst of all, the recital of the lecturer's own readily available book on the subject.

The other danger is to be short-sighted and to label everything as useless unless its relevance is immediately clear. About 13% of university students fail or withdraw from their courses. In the majority of cases this is voluntary and takes place in the first year. It is significant, however, that the fewest failures or dropouts occur in courses where there is a strong motivation towards a particular professional career — medicine, dentistry, law, *etc*. This sort of relevance and concern presumably carries the weaker candidates through. For the Christian the motivation is even stronger, because he is confident that his studies are part of God's will, which is good and perfect and which has a future in view. He never wastes our time or talents, and even the tedious can be useful in forming character and deepening trust.

Exams

No chapter on academic work would be complete without some thoughts on the subject of exams. In many colleges at present they seem to be going out of fashion in favour of a system of continuous assessment. In many ways, of course, this is much fairer. The exam system of 'stand and deliver' against the clock means that other factors besides knowledge and intellectual ability are being tested. While there may be value in that, it hardly ensures that everyone starts on equal ground.

The inbuilt disadvantage with continuous assessment seems to be that the agony is prolonged over the whole course. Every major piece of work counts, which places considerable strain on students all the time, and two or three poor grades can lead to despair. We live in an imperfect world and so we must face up to assessment as being a necessary evil, though I must confess that in the dentist's chair, for example, I am quite glad that there are standards and exams he has passed! So the sensible thing seems to be to recognize that the exams or some other form of assessment will come, and to begin planning well in advance accordingly. They can even become a useful stimulus to work, in that the eventual outcome is largely dependent upon how thoroughly the work has been done over the year.

Probably most students who suffer from anxiety over exams are prone to working too much, rather than too little. The danger of overwork is that we are exhausted when the exams arrive and so unable to do our best. Others find themselves unable to revise because of their numbing discouragement at the very thought of exams coming. This is often coupled with sleeplessness, and in such cases one should certainly not be reticent in seeking advice from a tutor or doctor. Coping with other people's exams can sometimes be more demanding than one's own, but there is a great deal that can be done to help other students who are worried, just by listening and sharing their problems, or by going off together for a day or afternoon, to get right away from work.

Revision is a very personal matter, which we each need to plan out to suit ourselves. It is a good idea to begin in the vacation before the exams and to plan some sort of coverage of the material over the coming term. In fact if you have the discipline to do it, the vacations are an ideal time for catching up on incomplete work, revising and reviewing progress. A couple of hours work a day during the vacs can do a great deal to keep the wheels turning. Most people find that they remember best the things they write down, but we all develop our own methods of recall and there are plenty of books available on methods of study. Probably for most of us a steady build-up achieves more than the frantic last-minute sprint, both in confidence and performance, so that a regular diet of increasing doses of revision seems to yield the best results. Past papers are of course very valuable in ensuring not only that you know the facts but that you can use them flexibly.

Exams are a time of strain, not least when you live in hall with several hundred other people who are tense. But from the Christian point of view they are a time of witness and growth. We believe in a sovereign God who is all-knowing, all-wise and who holds our lives in his almighty hand. We believe in prayer and enjoy an open access, through Christ, into God's presence. This, then, is a time when what we say we believe is demonstrably applied to a real-life situation. Our own faith can be strengthened and others will see the reality of God's help. Some have even come to trust Christ for themselves through the witness of Christians' lives at this critical time. And for the Christian student there is the very real confidence that, having worked conscientiously and done his very best, he can safely leave the result with God.

4 Are you 'religious'?

'Are you "religious"?' The question has been asked by countless new students spotting a Bible beside the bed of their new room-mate, and has met with a variety of responses from hasty denial to vigorous attack. It makes religion sound a bit like a disease, and of course mere religion can be pretty deathly. Yet it remains a talking point in student life, particularly in terms of the supernatural. Man, made in God's image, has an appetite for the spiritual which materialism will always leave unsatisfied and so it is not surprising to find widespread interest in spiritism and magic, meditation and yoga, and even in Indian gurus and mysticism.

You cannot be a secret Christian for long in the student world. Either your beliefs and way of life will mark you out as different, so that secrecy becomes unfeasible, or your faith will go underground until your Christianity is not just secret, but dead. Like Timothy, we are called on to 'follow the pattern of the sound words' and to 'guard the truth' (2 Tim. 1 : 13, 14). We have nothing to fear and certainly nothing to be ashamed of. As Christians we can humbly say that we know whom we have believed, that we have a message to pass on, a foundation on which to build; and in a society where there is an increasing hunger for spiritual reality we have an unparalleled opportunity to present the claims of the Lord Jesus Christ.

All this demands that our Christian faith is real and deep. It is no use reserving a special compartment of life, labelled 'Christianity', to which I devote part of my spare time, much as my friend will play the oboe, or go potholing — as an interesting leisure-time pursuit. This sort of half-heartedness is doomed to failure. If we are

Christians at all, we must be Christians in all. The primary fact about our life is that we belong to Christ, we have been bought with the price of his blood, and so the whole of life belongs to him and is to be lived in his strength, for his praise. In this realm, as in every other, we need to settle this basic attitude and deliberately focus our priorities, or we shall find events themselves dictating our choices.

God's family

One of the basic facts of Christian experience, on which we must reckon and build, is that we belong to the family of God and as such we are immediately related to other Christians. This is especially important when moving into a new situation, such as life at college. In the most fundamental sense every Christian is united to Christ who will neither fail us nor forsake us (Heb. 13:5). We can claim his help and strength in every situation.

The obvious development of this is that all who are united to Christ are through him united to one another. There is *one* body to which all Christian believers belong. 'So we, though many, are one body in Christ, and individually members one of another' (Rom. 12:5). Every Christian is a member of the universal church and our association with a particular local fellowship is an expression of that fact. So when a Christian leaves home to go to college, he is transferring from one branch of the family to another. He belongs to the 'gospel people' and that is where he will find his spiritual home and put down his roots. He knows that he can't go it alone in the Christian life, and so he will be eager to share fellowship with other Christians and to contribute his part to the upbuilding and functioning of the body of Christ in that place. This will not be peripheral in his scheme of things if he has realized that Christ is the source of all that matters most in his life. But where is fellowship like this to be found?

There are two main answers to that question — in the

local churches of the town where he is studying and in the Christian student groups on campus. They are neither exclusive alternatives nor competitors. In practice most Christian students find they benefit from, and contribute to, both. But of the two, if there is a primary loyalty, it must be to a local church, because this is the most representative manifestation of the body of Christ in that locality. Here is the family of God, representing a cross-section of ages, backgrounds, jobs and gifts, in a completeness which no student group by definition could begin to match. The church also provides a regular ministry of God's Word and of the sacraments, together with a pastoral concern and spiritual oversight, which would be inappropriate to a student group, besides being quite beyond the spiritual maturity of almost all student leaders. This is where any Christian moving into the locality belongs and the Christian student is not exempt by virtue of his being a student.

It is very easy moving all week in the narrow age-band of the student scene and dealing largely with academic and intellectual questions to become isolated from the mainstream of everyday life in the world. Problems can become magnified out of all proportion on campus and tensions can build up because of the artificial atmosphere of student life. We need the earthing that a local church gives us, in the real world, as well as the fresh air which being in worship with a wider group of people and sitting under a less student-orientated teaching of Scripture can bring us week by week. A student group alone can quickly become ingrown.

But there are difficulties about settling in to a local church in this way. It takes time, and if you have come from a very warm home church where you know everybody, even the friendliest of new places can seem a bit cold by comparison at first. It may even be difficult to find a church at all like the one at home. Sometimes it is fashionable among students to be spiritual nomads and to wander from church to church 'seeking pasture'. There is something in the argument that student life provides a rare opportunity to worship in churches of denominations other than your own and to broaden your experience of different ways of worship. But this must be with a view to settling in one church eventually. It is fraught with dangers as a policy, because it can lead to an attitude of sermon-tasting, where preacher is compared with preacher, until no-one quite comes up to standard and the hearer has lost all sense of sitting under the authority of God's Word and is spiritually impervious as a result. We all need a regular weekly diet of consecutive biblical teaching and this should be one of our prime considerations in choosing a church. Go where the congregation is taught the Bible in a lively, applied way and you will almost always find the warmth of Christian love and fellowship generated among them.

Having made your choice, you may still find it hard to be involved, or to know how much to try to be involved. For one thing, a student is there for only half the year and it may be almost impossible to take on any regular commitments, such as teaching in the Sunday school. Some churches, though these are comparatively rare, have overcome this by dove-tailing arrangements with their own student members during vacations. But, although you won't have the continuity of involvement of a full-time job at this stage, you can still be a lot of use. It is important to have a sense of loyalty to the fellowship and to try to be there regularly on Sunday. A few churches arrange for students studying in the town to become associate members during term-time, which helps to strengthen the links. They are eligible to attend church business meetings, receive information about all the church activities and in turn pledge their support in prayer for the church leaders and members and in giving. But for most students it will be a case of involvement on Sundays and perhaps at a mid-week prayer meeting. The latter may be more accessible when the church is in an area of student digs, where the main university or college is perhaps several miles away and students automatically feel more a part of the locality than of the student life. Certainly there is no place like the prayer meeting for real involvement in the life of the church.

Students living at home will of course face the opposite adjustment of knowing how far to detach themselves from all the church meetings and immerse themselves in campus life. Most become nine-to-five workers at college and hardly ever become involved in student society at all, which seems a pity. It can be an escape from the demands of witnessing in the student context to concentrate all one's energies into the local church.

One area which highlights this tension is the use of Sunday. It is very easy for Sunday to become a round of almost ceaseless activity, with hardly any time for rest or recreation. This is especially a danger where a student Christian Union runs a Sunday programme which is fitted around that of the local churches. If we establish the basic principle of no academic work on Sunday, then the day is set free to be 'holy' — separate for God's use. At least part of that use is worship, so that every Christian should be worshipping somewhere in a community of God's people at some time on every Sunday. The other part of its use is the sabbath rest of which the Bible often speaks. Clearly this refers primarily to rest from our regular work, but it may be right to use part of the day to catch up on the sleep debt of a very heavy week. What is not condoned is laziness, or the worldliness which drifts purposelessly through the day because everyone else in hall lives like that. If it is in one sense especially the Lord's day, then we must consult him about its use, and we shall find that a constructive attitude towards our time will bring a refreshment which renews us in every way for the new week beginning.

Student Christian groups

What, then, is the place of the student group, as distinct from the local church? The college, or campus, is the environment in which the student spends most of his time, where he makes his closest friends, often where he eats and sleeps as well as works. As such it must be the primary focus of our Christian witness. Local churches usually find it hard to carry out a specific ministry to students. A few of their members may open their homes, or even visit student residences, but in order to penetrate the university or college, the church would usually have to mount a special 'missionary' operation. This would be quite foolish if there were already members living and working in that area, as is, of course, the case.

Christian students are therefore called to be witnesses among their fellows-students, first and foremost, as a missionary arm of the wider church. If we do not take our responsibilities seriously to witness to Christ at college, then no-one else will do it for us; the student world will be unevangelized. The Bible teaches that we are first to penetrate the environment we are in and then perhaps to spread out more widely. It does seem right that we should devote most of our time to this very open area for the short period of time in which we are students, especially in view of the enormous potential for the spread of the gospel represented by the student world. It can be tough and there are temptations not to devote as much time to our student friends as we should. It may be more exciting to run an open-air down town, or to help in a local youth club, than to spend an evening talking with a non-Christian friend down the corridor and trying to come to grips with his difficult questions and probing arguments. The same is true in terms of social work. It may be much more costly to become involved with a chronically touchy person in your seminar group, than to spend an evening a week decorating old age pensioners' homes, or working among down and outs. All these activities are excellent, and because one is harder than another does not mean it is better or more important. Clearly we must all examine our motives and make sure that, whatever else we do, we are not running away from our responsibility to live as Christians where we are. It will depend on how large the Christian body is in a given place, on how great the need is and so on, but we must not neglect our 'Jerusalem' because it looks more attractive to work in Samaria and beyond (Acts 1 : 8).

In student life, ideas can spread very rapidly and there is an open opportunity to talk about anything. People are probably more willing to consider Christianity than they will be at any other time in their lives. Many Christians coming to college for the first time are very surprised by this openness of other students to think seriously about Christian things and to consider the claims of the Lord Jesus Christ. This is in marked contrast to the attitudes found in many sixth forms, where the climate is often one of cosy closed-mindedness to spiritual things. But certainly we have no need to be timid or apprehensive in our Christian witness. Generally it is true that fellow-students are less hostile and far more willing to talk than we imagine they will be. Outside the student world there may be more truth in the poster outside a church which proclaimed, 'Most people's minds are like concrete; thoroughly mixed and permanently set.' But it is rare to find such entrenched attitudes among students, and so we must seize the opportunities.

Students from all over the world, many of whom have never really heard of Christ, are literally on our doorstep. Many of these students from overseas find life here exceedingly impersonal and unfriendly. Our traditional 'reserve' vies with the weather to provide the more chilling welcome. All too often when there is an enthusiastic welcome in the first few days of term, it is followed by complete lack of interest in them when once the initial contacts are over. An enormous opportunity exists here for Christian students to show genuine love and friendship. For many students from abroad this will be their first encounter with vital Christianity. It may be virtually impossible for them to hear the gospel clearly explained in their home land, or to discuss it with intelligent Christians, yet in the student scene over here such possibilities abound.

Most overseas students are far more friendly than we are and are delighted to make personal contact. Anything that we can give in terms of welcome, help and friendship will be repaid over and over again by the warmth of a new friendship and personal insights into another society and culture. They are unlikely to be directly influenced by the local churches because they do not meet their members, and when they have left college or university their ideas will be much more fixed and their leisure to think much reduced. The student world provides a great opportunity to gossip the gospel (Acts 8:4) for which every Christian student is needed for as much time as he can possibly give.

There are several Christian societies in most colleges and universities. Some of these are denominational, linked to specific churches in the town, or having their own chaplains and centres on campus. In most places they are brought together by an ecumenical committee, which arranges some joint meetings and co-ordinates the work of the various chaplains, though each society also runs an independent programme. Sometimes there will be weekly study/discussion groups and almost always a Sunday afternoon or evening fellowship centred on the college chapel or a town church. Many Christians belong to both a denominational and an interdenominational group. In some places there is more than one evangelical agency at work, such as Navigators or Campus Crusade for Christ, but almost everywhere the interdenominational Christian Unions are now the main Christian society and among the largest of all the student societies.

The Christian Unions are student-led societies which have developed spontaneously over several decades as Christians have come together to help one another to live and witness in the student world. Just as the individual Christian's aim is to glorify God in obedience and love, so the Union exists to help and encourage its members

42

to that end. Its main purpose is the witness to, and proclamation of, the basic truths of biblical Christianity throughout the student body. It exists both to hold fast to a basic framework of revealed truth and to hold forth that truth, the Word of life, to others (Phil. 2:16). The unifying factor among its members is truth, which is why membership is dependent upon a personal confession of faith in Jesus Christ as Saviour, Lord and God. He is the Truth, and spiritual unity is found only in a personal commitment to Christ, which in turn implies a personal witness to the fundamental truths of the Christian faith as revealed in the Bible. In order to do this the Christian Union's activities are designed to enable members to advance in their understanding of the Christian faith and to grow in character and consistency. It does not exist as an end in itself but as a means to the end of greater maturity of Christian life and character among its members and an increasingly widespread penetration of the college or university with the Christian message.

As a student, it is important to see that your faith is developing by being stretched and that you are being trained as a disciple. This means growing as an individual and not being moulded into a Christian Union stereotype. Social pressures to conform exist as much within a Christian society as elsewhere, and there is a danger in an active and thriving Christian Union of trying to live up to a 'brand image' of what the keen Christian is and does, which is often little more than imitation of someone who is respected by all the group. This can find its expression in the number of meetings one is tacitly expected to attend (or not attend, according to taste!), or in vocabulary, dress, outward enthusiasm and so on. This is a mark of immaturity, but so is the extravagant reaction into which we can easily be tempted, when all the current shibboleths are deliberately flouted. This sort of thing tends to develop when we become too concerned about the Christian Union, and imagine that God is glorified by sound machinery rather than by men and women walking in obedience to him, in the Spirit. The very institution of a Christian Union, accepted as a thriving student society, could well be more dangerous to its life than any attacks from without, unless the personal walk with God and growth in maturity of each individual Christian is kept absolutely central to its purpose.

Studying the Bible and praying together

This is why the Bible must always be the core of the Christian Union's programme. Regular meetings at which the Bible is explained and applied provide invaluable foundations for Christian growth. A great deal can also be learnt from studying the Bible with other students in a small group, once a week, and many have found this a revolutionizing experience. It is always stimulating to have other minds working on the same passage and to be able to share difficulties and new insights with one another.

Satisfying groups like this do not, of course, appear out of the blue. They have to be worked at and persevered with. Sometimes students become disillusioned because the study has become coldly academic and dry, or because relationships between members of the group are not so open and warm-hearted as they might be. The temptation in a situation like that is to opt out, or to change the function of the group from Bible study to the vaguer 'fellowship'. Neither seems to be a remedy. The latter usually ends in a sharing of personal experiences which has some encouragement value, but cannot feed the spiritual life as the Bible does, and which is anyway subject to the law of diminishing returns. A group which becomes over-concerned about its fellowship is likely to become increasingly introverted and to find itself pursuing an increasingly elusive ideal. Fellowship, like happiness, is a by-product, in this case of studying, working and witnessing together. The answer is not so much in abandoning Bible study but in improving it. This means each group member regarding it as important, preparing adequately, praying regularly and expecting God to teach him through it. For his own part he will avoid the sort of red herrings and irrelevant controversies that make the group time one of pooling ignorance. Instead he will recognize the mutual responsibility within the group membership to expose one another to what the Bible actually says, and if it is real *Bible* study everyone will benefit.

The cement of a Bible study group is the time of praying together, in which true fellowship develops as lessons are prayed home, personal needs raised and the wider work of God throughout the world remembered. In some of the larger Christian Unions there are special missionary prayer-study groups which meet weekly or fortnightly to become acquainted with the particular needs and opportunities of God's work in one specific country or continent. Membership of one of these groups can be a marvellous way of enlarging your own spiritual horizons and really getting involved in the world-wide church. There may also be a regular prayer group meeting in your hall to which you can go. Obviously the point is not to notch up as many attendances at meetings as possible, but to give as many opportunities for Christian growth and service as each individual needs and can take. You can go to too many meetings (as is often pointed out) but you can also go to too few.

It is of crucial importance that Christians within a college situation regularly pray together. There is something wrong with any Christian group that does not regard its prayer meeting as the first priority. If you go to nothing else the Christian Union puts on, go to your group prayer meeting. You will soon learn the value of the other activities there! This is where together you can work out what God's plan is for your witness in the area for which you are responsible. Here you can pray for your work, friends, family and church. Many Christians have learnt to pray in meetings like these and have found their faith immeasurably strengthened. There are special promises in the Bible for Christians who pray together

(Mt. 18:19, 20; Jn. 14:13) and it is a great thrill to see God answering specific requests. Some groups have kept a requests book with a column for answers received, so that praise can mingle with intercession. All this may be unfamiliar to you, but it is really the most natural thing in the world for Christians to do together and you will find a great deal of personal encouragement in doing it. You belong in the family, talking to the Father.

These are all unique opportunities for Christian fellowship and service which many Christians have found to be a formative influence in their own experience of God and valuable training for his service after they leave college or university. Of course, any close group can easily develop into a clique and we must be alive to the dangers inherent in a 'holy huddle' which are sometimes more apparent to our critics than to us. The Christian will always be involved in this tension of living in this world as a citizen of another one, and the balance which we need to achieve in student life is simply transferring the same battle to a new terrain. Everything depends upon the spiritual health of the individual Christians and our personal walk with God. To rely on a strong fellowship as a substitute for a personal relationship with God is disastrous, both because the watching world is confirmed in its view that Christianity is a cosy club for the emotionally inadequate and because the hollowness of the individual will inevitably be exposed when he or she leaves college. We need rather to recognize that the whole point of a fellowship is that it consists of people walking with God, finding others along the same road, and encouraging each other to keep going.

On your own?

Of course you may find yourself in a college or an annexe where there is no organized Christian witness at all. Some of the shorter-course colleges have such a rapid turnover of students that a Christian Union may exist one year and not the next, unless new students are prepared to take the initiative in getting something started. Perhaps you are in college for only one or two days a week, and trying to find another Christian may seem like looking for a needle in a haystack.

What can be done? The answer is a great deal if *you* are prepared to do it, prayerfully and perseveringly. You can find out from reception or the Students Union whether there has been a Christian group within living memory and whether there are any survivors to contact. They may also know of any Christian lecturers or administrative staff who might be willing to help. Then probably the best idea is to put up as large and striking a notice as possible inviting anybody who knows they are a Christian, or who has an interest in finding out and discussing what the Bible has to say, to a meeting at a specific time and place. Often this has produced a surprisingly good and enthusiastic response and has been the means of starting a lively witness in that college.

There are full-time travelling secretaries of the Inter-College Christian Fellowship who visit in your area and who would be delighted to call in and advise you on how to help set up an active group, with a useful programme and outreach.[1] So don't despair if you seem to be the only Christian around; see it rather as a key opportunity prayerfully to think about setting up a witness in your new missionary situation.

Daily contact with God

Much of what has been said depends upon our daily contact with God in prayer and Bible study. Nothing is of greater importance for spiritual survival and effectiveness. And in spite of our feelings to the contrary, life as a student is an ideal setting in which to cultivate the habit.

The first thing is to settle on a regular time of day in which deliberately to meet with God. There is nothing magical about the morning, though it seems ideal before meeting the demands of the day to go through it, in

[1] Write to ICCF, 39 Bedford Square, London WC1B 3EY.

thought and prayer, with God. Many Christians over many years have discovered the immense value of starting each day with the Lord. But if you are a night bird with nine o'clock lectures you may find that your life-style cannot support it. You must then decide whether or not to change your life-style and make it a rule to go to bed eight hours before you need to get up. Some students use their lunchtime (though this limits your contacts) while others prefer the time before the evening meal. Last thing at night seldom succeeds and Christians who fall asleep on their knees after twelve are rarely up to much the next day.

Each of us must find his own pattern. It may mean being disciplined in leaving your coffee and inconsequential Christian chatter early. Not a bad idea anyway! But it should not mean leaving a talk with a troubled Christian or interested non-Christian. There is a particularly lively nocturnal culture among students and some people open up most late at night. We must each be settled in our own minds about the best time, but reckon that it will need effort and be a constant battle to keep it free. Make your own rules, but make them realistically, to be kept. There are several helpful books on personal prayer and Bible study which suggest methods and aids;[2] my purpose here is to stress its necessity. Like breathing, it matters!

This daily relationship with God is what transforms life for the Christian. As I recognize the privilege of living each day with the Lord, I begin to see people through Christ's eyes and to live the life God designed me for. This liberates me from seeing evangelism as an activity by which the unenlightened are sprayed, at arm's length,

[2] Basic books in these areas include J. D. C. Anderson (ed.), *The Quiet Time* (IVP); John R. W. Stott, *Understanding the Bible* (Scripture Union); John B. Job (ed.), *Studying God's Word* (IVP); and O. Hallesby, *Prayer* (IVP). For a systematic course of daily Bible study, designed to cover the whole Bible in three years, IVP produces *Search the Scriptures,* in three paperback volumes or one hardback edition. This is especially geared to students.

with the gospel, or thinking of witness in terms of a 'hit-and-run' raid. In contrast, I shall begin to understand more of what Paul meant when he wrote to the young church at Thessalonica, 'Because of our love for you we were ready to share with you not only the Good News from God, but even our own lives' (1 Thes. 2:8, TEV).

Spending time with God enables me to become more human, not less, more like Jesus who could never be fitted into a neat man-made box. He was neither the hippy, nor the revolutionary. Neither the respectable working man nor the educated rabbi cap fits him exactly. What struck men was his relationship with the Father. The more we foster that relationship, the more we shall have to give to our fellow-students. Perhaps the greatest gift we can give to another person is ourselves, our time, our undivided attention, and paradoxically this may be where the Christian student is most doing Christ's will. And the more we foster our relationship with God, the more we are able to work out the common aim of the Christian Union. Paul's aim was to 'present every man mature in Christ' (Col. 1:28) or again, to build up the body of Christ, 'until we all attain to the unity of the faith and of the knowledge of the Son of God, to mature manhood, to the measure of the stature of the fulness of Christ' (Eph. 4:12, 13). This means knowing what we believe and why, working out the Bible's teaching in every area of life, constantly bringing our own lives under its examination, applying its commands in action and seeking God's Spirit to work in us, to make each one the fully developed individual God created us to be.

It will teach us to respect the individuality of our fellow-Christians too. There are weaknesses and strengths in all of us, elements to be developed and others to be suppressed, but God does not necessarily turn the shy, retiring person into a hearty extrovert. We must beware of forcing ourselves to be what we are not, either because we wish we were different, or because we are under pressure to conform to other people's images. We are not to force our experiences on to everyone else, to insist on a uniformity of personality among Christians which is totally alien to the liberty of the gospel.

Nor are we to go beyond the clear teaching of the Bible and try to enforce a controversial doctrinal interpretation or personal experience upon other members of the Christian Union. The fellowship exists for the defence and spread of the gospel, not to be swung from one doctrinal controversy to another by over-dominant personalities. We shall learn to value the infinite variety which God has built into his church in making us all different, to respect differences of opinion over less than central issues, to agree to differ in love and not to think of ourselves more highly than we ought to think. It is a healthy discipline to belong to as imperfect a group of Christians as the average Christian Union, not least because we are brought to worship God for the immensity of his grace in bothering with people like us.

R. J. Mowll wrote to the student generation of forty years ago: 'The greatest witness you can give as an undergraduate is that of a life devoted to the fulfilment of God's purposes for you. If he has called you to be a doctor, do not make the mistake of thinking either that he wants you to be a second-rate one, or that a doctor needs only his knowledge of the medical art ... God has not guided you to go to a university in order that you may do there those things which can be done elsewhere.'

We need the same reminder. Find out the area in which God has called you to serve during your college career. Seize the unique opportunities while you have them and serve God with all your might.

5 People and problems

It is sad, but true, that many students become disillusioned with their experience of life at college. Sometimes this is a matter of personality. They may be of the temperament that is quickly disappointed by anything routine, and people like this are apt to discover that life away from college when they leave is even worse! But if you ask where this disappointment finds its roots, their dissatisfaction is nearly always expressed in the area of personal relationships. The staff are not as stimulating and forward-looking as they should be; other students are bourgeois, apathetic and dull. Often the deepest cause is within the individual's own personality with which he is struggling to come to terms.

In some cases, the college or university becomes an intense focus of the problems which face society at large. There are the enormous dilemmas produced by man's own technology — nuclear warfare, the population explosion, the abuse or pollution of the earth's resources, the instant 'culture' of the mass media — to which so much of what happens at college seems quite irrelevant. The optimism of the pundits that more education, more research, or more money and ingenuity can solve everybody's problems begins to have a hollow ring in many students' ears. Moreover, the prevailing philosophy that life is without meaning and the universe a gigantic accident, so that life itself has become a sick joke, seems to reinforce the despair and disgust which permeates the cultural atmosphere of our generation. It is not surprising that many people who stop to think are aware of an acute sense of frustration, as the individual faces the seemingly insurmountable problems of society. What sort of a dent can one man possibly hope to make? And so often the course work in a student's particular subject seems increasingly detailed and obscure, until he really does seem to know more and more about less and less.

But at the same time, over against the tyranny of the machine and the facelessness of the computerized society, there is a defiant awareness of the value of individual personality. People do matter; and as Christians we know why. There is a personal God who creates each one and who is infinitely concerned for every individual. For our non-Christian friends, however, there is only the intuitive feeling that people ought to matter, diluted by the nagging fear that they do not, and that there is no real reason (as opposed to feeling) why they should.

On many college campuses, and in the youth culture generally, there is something of a revolt against the rational and scientific, and a strong move, generated by an emotional over-reaction, back to the instinctive and 'natural', which often means the primitive and unrealistic. The individual must assert himself against the system. It is a sound human instinct, alive and very much kicking in today's student world. A paragraph from one of the Underground press productions, *Gandalf's Garden*, speaks representatively when it records: 'The angry young men are still angry, but with the anger flows a new wave of gentle feeling, seeking expression in self-realization. The more self-knowing a person can become, the more beautiful he or she will become from the deep roots. We influence others by what we are ourselves. It is not even necessary to "do" but merely to "become" . . . Good vibrations are catching.'

So there is a tendency to want to dig deeper into the personality, in order to find meaning. Many of the arts and social sciences have an increasing element of self-discovery woven into their courses. But the end-product often proves to be simply an intensified sense of disappointment. How can one's inner resources be developed? Where is reality to be found?

To many there seems to exist at the end of the search simply a vacuum, which Christians recognize as the God-shaped blank in the human personality. We would agree that 'being' matters most, but it will inevitably issue in action, words, involvement with others. The problem is how a deeper awareness of oneself can lead to a fuller life, unless there is also implicit within the discovery a new dynamic to change you and make you the person you want to be. Only the Holy Spirit can bring about such a miracle in a man's life and it is at this very level that he seems to be communicating to so many students today.

For those who become Christians while they are students it is often seeing Christ in another student's life which begins their search. Not the 'being' in isolation — but the inner life translated into activity, into relationships. 'He had something that I hadn't got, and I was intrigued to find out what made him like that.' A Christian's personal relationships are a vital part of his life at college. 'They seemed to have such a love for other people.' The story could be repeated a thousand times. So in this chapter we shall look at some of the aspects of this crucial area of experience, as part of our attempt to become more fully Christian.

Relationships with parents

It makes a great difference, as you launch out into life away from home, if your base is a stable one within your own family. If you have been used to living away from home, at school, you will probably have had to sort this out already, but for those who leave home for the first time when they go to college, there will be a number of new adjustments to both parents and family. The late teens produce their own tensions at home as we each have to assert our individuality and convince our parents that we really have grown up. In some ways this sort of caring family environment is the best preparation for student life, though over-protection is suffocating. But many students have never been privileged to experience a

53

stable home life and will lack the security which a strong base can provide. All of us will have developed certain inner resources and, however good or bad our relationships with the family are, they usually prove to be more predictable than any other, and in that sense provide a firmer footing.

If you are the first student in your family, you may find yourself treated to a curious mixture of pride and scepticism about your achievement. The student world as it is presented by the media is usually in the most garish colours, implying that it is all beads and weeds, or beer and immorality, so that parents might be forgiven for viewing it with somewhat jaundiced eyes. Christian parents are often excessively worried about the influences the student world will bring to bear on their children; nor is this without justification. There may be a feeling in your family that academic work is very detached from the real business of living — an ivory tower. You may still be considered not quite 'normal' as you are not yet self-supporting financially, or contributing to the family income. From the student side we must face the fact that it is easy to appear detached, even remote, from the family. This can be interpreted as aloofness, but it is really perplexity to know where, if at all, we now fit in at home. Sometimes helping out financially by getting a job during the vacations can help to restore sagging confidence and rebuild a positive relationship.

For some students, however, the opposite is the case, and you may feel under a different sort of parental pressure. Higher education has become a social commodity and there may be a good deal of kudos involved at home in your getting to college and doing well there. It can be quite shattering to parents whose lives have been tacitly devoted to getting on and making a success of life, in conventional terms, to find their children suddenly infected with the *laissez-faire*, anti-success mood of the times. The Christian student does not see success (in terms of examination results) as the sole end of his study.

54

We have to sort out our own priorities and goals, and while this will inevitably involve us in doing our very best in our work, it will not be to the exclusion of everything else.

Here, as in every other relationship, the important thing to remember is the essential need to talk things out frankly. This is a central point in our witness if we are committed Christians and our parents are not. Often they will interpret our faith (especially when it is new) as a vote of no confidence in their whole style and basis of life. Indeed it is, because if they are to become Christians, they will in effect be admitting that their lives have been built on quite the wrong foundation up to this time. It's not easy to be taught something like that by your own child. We must do all we can to explain and discuss, so that they see both the reality of our faith and its practice, in everyday family terms.

For the Christian student the principle 'Honour your father and mother' must always be fundamental and binding. This is not the same thing as a slavish obedience to their every whim and fancy and it is certainly not intended to decrease an individual's independence. It finds its origin in a right attitude towards God, as the heavenly Father, whom we seek to love with heart, mind and strength. This will in turn make it easier, not harder, to honour our parents. That same love will be thoughtful for their interests and feelings, will remember their help and sacrifices and will above all try to understand and share the new experiences and areas of interest in one's student life.

Between the sexes

Many students find that the relationship which has most meaning for them while they are at college is with a particular friend or friends of the opposite sex. Here college life is very little different from that of young people of the same age group anywhere, except that at college a couple probably have more time to spend with

55

one another, especially if they are on the same course. Certainly they are unlikely to see as much of one another in ordinary married life! The modern world sees one answer to its problems of personal identity and meaning in romantic love, and the student scene mirrors this. The Christian, too, recognizes that human love is one of God's greatest blessings in life and has no time for a negative attitude, but he also recognizes that no other human being can provide an individual with a total purpose for living and so he does not expect to find his satisfaction here, unless both partners are joined together by a deep love for God. How, then, is a Christian to think of the whole confused area of love, sex and marriage in the student world?

The Bible is never negative in its approach. It uses the whole area of relationships based on marriage and the family as an illustration of some of the great truths about our relationship to God. His Fatherhood is the pattern or ideal of all human fatherhood, seen in his relationship to us as his children. Paul uses the relationship of the bridegroom to his bride as a picture of Christ's relationship to the church, both now and at the end of time.

God clearly regards sexual love and its consummation in marriage and family life as one of the most wonderful gifts in creation. We need to remember that it is *his* creation ('It is not good that the man should be alone', Gn. 2:18) and it is therefore good. This helps us to see sex as something far greater than its physical expression alone. It is sad that in our society not only has 'love' been devalued as a word, but even the term 'sex' has come to mean only the physical act, often with hints of immorality. Sex was made for marriage and the family; that is its ultimate goal. Yet we all benefit from the social relationships between the sexes which enrich life, but stop far short of marriage or any physical expression. The problem today is that because the physical side of sex is emphasized to the exclusion of almost every other aspect, we too easily assume that this is the main, or only, con-

56

sideration and rush headlong into physical relationships, which can be quite wrong personally and morally. Promiscuity and free love may be a logical outcome of the reasoning that man is nothing but an animal, but because we know that God has created him as something far more than that we must beware of buying our society's current set of fashionable lies.

Even in strong Christian friendships it is easy to respond to the pressures of society around us by pushing things too quickly along the path of physical expression, and losing the best part of such friendships because the physical side has come to dominate the relationship in a way that is out of all proportion. Sex is too great a gift for us to allow it to be abused like this. It is so much deeper in the exchange of ideas, the differences and complementarity of outlook, and the sheer enjoyment of friendship. As Christians we want to keep to the boundaries God has ordained, in order that we may be truly free to enjoy his best for us. These are neither negative nor legalistic, though even if they were that would not be an argument for doing away with them. We are not to misrepresent the goodness of our God who has set these moral landmarks for our positive good, because he knows, as our Creator, that we are not infinitely adaptable.

We shall want to claim then that Christian morality arises out of the way in which God has made us. We are not to commit fornication because it is a sin against the body (1 Cor. 6:18) and it therefore follows that we are not to commit adultery (Ex. 20:14) which is in addition a sin against an innocent third party. God's principle is that sexual intercourse is to be confined to marriage, else the basis of life-long monogamous marriage and with it the family will be overthrown. In fact to defy the rules is to defy the Creator, to sin against the way he has chosen to make us, as Paul goes on to point out in 1 Corinthians 6:19, 20, where he teaches that our bodies belong by right of creation to God. This is the anchor of the

Christian's position as taught throughout the Bible.

It will be argued against it that if a couple are really in love and intend to marry, it cannot be wrong. But if they are so committed to one another as to enter the deepest bond by this irreversible action, then the logical step is marriage, not fornication. Why are they not prepared to be married publicly and irreversibly? If they are not ready for that then they are not ready for physical union. Indeed to snatch God's gift before his time often leads in effect to the weakening of the relationship, because its motivation is basically the selfish one of pleasure-centred possession, whereas true love gives unselfishly and that indicates restraint, not licence. So often marriages go wrong because the basis of the relationship at the deepest level has always been selfish, seeking personal satisfaction: What can I get out of it? And this has never really been admitted and faced up to; it has been passed off as 'love'.

In the student world where everybody needs to belong to someone, we need to be especially aware of forming deep attachments for the wrong reasons. It is so easy to want to satisfy our own needs, rather than love our partner unselfishly, but this is the pagan concept of sex as self-gratification. Our desires to belong can be fulfilled by a whole range of friendships and groups; but they are no foundation on which to build the most intimate life-long relationship.

There are also some strong social pressures in the college situation, however. In many places everything is done in couples socially and it can be very embarrassing and unsettling not to have a regular boy- or girl-friend. You can even come to believe that you are quite abnormal not to be tied up with someone. Christians have differing views about this. Some would see the ideal as one steady friend — the one you eventually marry. Others see advantages in dating a number. The important thing is we should be prepared to think this through and to enter all our relationships with sincerity and in self-awareness.

58

Make sure that each partner is quite sure where the other stands and how the other sees it.

Sometimes pressures occur because general relations between the sexes in the Christian Union are not as natural and open as they should be. It has been remarked that Paul's instruction to Timothy is to treat the younger women as sisters (1 Tim. 5:2) not as lepers! It is not unknown for Christian men to be guilty of an unloving and unchristian separation in a misdirected effort to keep clear of any sort of misunderstanding. This can lead Christian girls to accept invitations from non-Christian men in sheer desperation.

While there are cases of men becoming Christians through friendships with Christian girls, and *vice versa*, it is not a normal means of evangelism. We have to recognize, in any relationship with a non-Christian which is deepening, that it cannot lead to marriage if we are going to obey God (2 Cor. 6:14), and it may lead to personal frustration and spiritual decline. There are many marriages where the Christian wife married her husband only after his profession of faith. This became a pre-requisite for marriage which he was quite prepared to accept because of his love for the wife, but which was soon renounced when once the marriage had taken place. It may sound a hard thing to say, but it is true that if you marry a child of the devil you may expect to have trouble with your father-in-law.

Relations between the sexes in a Christian Union should be as open and free as possible, so as to allow one to partner (or ask to partner) another without embarrassment. Unfortunately some regard it as the ideal marriage bureau and mark their passage with a trail of broken hearts (at least temporarily) and disappointments. This is an area in which we may make many mistakes, and in which we especially need the protection of prayer, which forces us to be honest before God. It is important that we realize that commitment cannot be lightly entered or withdrawn in this area.

The last thing we want to do is to become problem-centred in our thinking about love and marriage. So many books abound and so much advice is everywhere available that there is a tendency to reduce the wonderful experience of falling in love to a list of rules, precepts and techniques. Yet the decision you make concerning a life partner will be one of the most important you will ever make and it would be foolish not to think hard and pray thoroughly about it. Christian marriage is worth waiting for; we want to be the best we can be for each other, and so we must give consideration to those situations which could lead us away from God's best. We have to know ourselves and our own weaknesses and not put ourselves in positions where they are most exposed and we are most vulnerable.

For example, it is increasingly the fashion among students to live in mixed houses or flats. Some Christians have gone along with this and found themselves under considerable pressures. We must be realistic before God about these things and not imagine that because we are Christians we are any less human, or not susceptible to exactly the same emotions and drives as any other man or woman. There is no point in opening the lion's jaw, placing your head inside and then fervently praying that it will not be bitten off. Too many students (sadly Christians among them) have found too late that to expose themselves to unnecessary temptation in this realm is to ride a tiger.

As Christians, then, we can recognize thankfully that sexuality is God's good gift to man. It is a gift, in trust, to be used in God's way, not a gift by which we or others are used. Our main concern will be to submit this powerful desire to God for his control so that we do not spoil it by its misuse. We have high standards and we need to live them, rather than just placard them to others. If we believe that our standards are God-given norms which are good for society as a whole, then we shall use appropriate occasions to explain to others the reasoning behind them and to try to persuade them to adopt them too. It is not our place to be angry with those who have no such standards because they do not know their Maker, but we can try to introduce them to him and help them to see and experience the power which he provides to live differently.

Sadly, some people who have failed once in this area give up all standards, because they recognize that God's are so high they have no hope of attaining them. Some Christians have even allowed a moral lapse totally to undermine their faith. We may have to live with the consequences of our sin, but our gospel is a message of forgiveness, and we slander God's character if we imagine that failure in this area cuts us off from his blessing. There is always the way of repentance and the sure promises of cleansing and forgiveness which follow, so that we can be restored completely in our relationship with him, however badly we may have fallen.

Loneliness

To many students deeply satisfying personal relationships are not forthcoming and they are thrown back upon themselves, which often means the inner personal vacuum. Loneliness is perhaps the greatest disease of modern man and the student world does not escape. One university lecture room had carved on a desk the question, 'Why am I so lonely when there are 2,000 other people here?' You may be in the crowd and yet still not be able to find yourself.

Often this sense of alienation is a product of the philosophical conditioning of our society. Man is not at home in a feelingless, impersonal world. Just stop one evening instead of rushing out to see someone, sit down with yourself, nothing and no-one else, and be quiet. You'll find out what bad company you can be! We have to come to terms with this, for this is the true state of every man and how, at his most honest, every man sees himself. Man without God is lonely, because without God he has no

61

real significance or meaning. All that exists is the echo of his own cynicism. It should not surprise us if some of our student friends are deeply affected by this sort of thinking. A few may be in deep despair, even contemplating suicide. Others are generally depressed from time to time, as they alternate between the struggle of trying to find a personal identity and the emptiness of the life they are living. The majority manage a fairly optimistic outlook, even though it may be materialist in essence and basically hollow.

As Christians we have a responsibility to love our neighbour and to have a special concern for those in particular need. They do need love that is expressed in genuine friendship, and many a Christian student with an open door and listening ear has been able to help greatly when friends have been feeling low. Our concern will be for the highest good of those whom we know, if we really love them. Much can be done just by listening sympathetically and sharing one another's burdens. In acute cases, though, Christian love may mean recognizing that skilled medical help is needed and handing over at this point to those better equipped to cope. We must beware of doing harm through our own incompetence. Yet even when we cannot do anything noticeably practical to help, listening and giving our undivided attention can be the most effective way of loving the person for Christ's sake — and we can always pray.

Of course we ourselves are not immune as Christians from the ups and downs of ordinary life, from the changes in circumstances or mood which we tend to call 'depression'. The term covers such a variety of attitudes and experiences that its use has become somewhat devalued. Clinical depression is a subject on its own and one on which expert medical advice must be sought; but what about the everyday 'blues'? All of us have to learn to come to terms with the individual personality that is 'me' and to live with ourselves. By nature, some will be much more prone to extreme swings of temperament than the more placid types, and becoming a Christian will not necessarily alter that. But what it does often mean is that we tend to put a 'spiritual' construction on everything that happens to us. We can fall into the trap of interpreting every setback as a spiritual crisis.

Sometimes feeling depressed does have a genuine spiritual cause. It may be the direct result of some sin, in which case our remedy is to return to God, through our Lord Jesus Christ, to confess the sin which has created the barrier between us and God and to receive the forgiveness he offers. But often the reason is that we are labouring under misleading views of the Christian life which we have assimilated. We may have been told that any form of depression is wrong and unworthy in a Christian, that we are always to be happy and so feeling low is either a sign of being under a cloud of God's displeasure or a question mark against whether we are truly converted. We haven't realized that the Bible's joy is in who God is and what he has done and is doing ('Rejoice in the Lord always', Phil. 4:4), rather than a masochistic glee in adverse circumstances. James 1:2 exhorts, 'Count it all joy when you meet various trials,' not because they are necessarily good in themselves, but because of the steadfastness which they produce in Christian character.

Perhaps we had not realized the spiritual battle into which we have entered, and were unprepared for the attacks of Satan. We imagined that we should 'float to Heaven on flowery beds of ease', that everything would be marvellously simple once we had come to the Lord. Still others become depressed by the experience of what they see as constant defeat in the warfare. There has been some failure in their Christian life and the 'accuser of the brethren', always ready to seize the advantage, tempts them to think that such an evildoer could not possibly be a Christian at all. He insinuates that God's love will be withdrawn, that his mercy is available only to 'good boys' and we have put ourselves outside it. So often we become depressed because we forget who we are, in

Christ, and what God has done in and for us.

Elijah's depression under the broom-tree in 1 Kings 19, for example, seems to have been due to the fact that he was physically and emotionally exhausted after the great experiences of God's victory on Mount Carmel. Hungry, tired, dejected — God's remedy in his case was firstly food and sleep. A good deal of student anxiety and depression can be traced to the same deficiencies, burning the candle at both ends. It may be that there is an external cause of a temporary nature which will soon pass — an essay 'crisis', or a problem in the family. Sometimes it can come as reaction after a time of special blessing and acute awareness of the presence of God in one's life for good. The Lord may be teaching us to rely on his promises rather than on our experiences. Perhaps it may be a particularly strong attack of the devil, an intensification of the warfare which is the lot of every Christian. In one sense, the problem itself is less important than our reaction to it. The view of the Christian life as one unhindered calm is scarcely biblical. Peter speaks of times of heaviness and testing which are the means God uses to strengthen our faith and make us lean harder on him (1 Pet. 1 : 6, 7; 4 : 12-16). As Oswald Sanders puts it, the trials that God sends are his 'votes of confidence in us'.

In such a situation it is usually helpful to go and talk it over with a friend, to pray together about it, or to have a complete break of activity, to do something physically rather than mentally demanding, or just to catch up on sleep. We have to get to know ourselves and not be afraid to accept what we find — warts and all. There is much that we can learn to do as our own spiritual doctor, applying the remedies of faith to the personal symptoms that we each recognize in ourselves. But if the trouble persists we should never despise those whose pastoral experience or medical knowledge may be able to help us greatly.

Another subject which may have implications for the Christian in his relationships with other students is that of drugs. This is an increasingly common problem in schools too. Often it begins by taking stimulants to improve work performance for examinations, or because certain drugs are said to expand the individual's consciousness. A Christian student cannot afford to be ignorant of the problem, especially as the lobby to legalize the smoking of cannabis becomes more vocal in the colleges. We must distinguish the types of drugs and their effects.

There are the barbiturates (*e.g.* purple hearts, French blues) which are strongly addictive physically and have effects very like alcohol, while the amphetamines (*e.g.* bennies, dexies, speed) give excitement and 'kick' and are psychologically addictive. The hallucinogens, such as cannabis (pot) and LSD (acid), vary in their effects. Cannabis produces excitement followed by drowsiness, but its effects are unpredictable. Some would argue that it can produce brain damage, and certainly its prolonged use leads to apathy and lack of interest in life generally. LSD produces hallucinations, mixing of the senses and can produce permanent brain damage. Heroin (morphine, opium) produces strong psychological addiction which it is difficult to cure in the long term. The person is so radically changed that he cannot exist without the drug. There is a good deal of detailed written material available on these aspects of the drugs.

The practical issue is how to recognize the problem and help the individual. Jim Cowley, in a paper for private circulation, made the following observations. It is very difficult to recognize an addict or drug-taker, but some indication is a person acting in unusual ways, his social group changing to the known or suspected drug-takers. He may be subject to exaggerated mood changes, or even to complete changes of character. His behaviour may vary between very active, extrovert, and dreamy, nonsensical reactions. In helping drug-takers it is essential to draw alongside them as a friend. This is a long-term work and it needs time to establish confidence in the relationship and to listen to and understand the person behind the mask. It is not helpful at this stage to consider it as a moral problem and to introduce categories of right and wrong, but rather to find out the cause of the drug-taking and to suggest alternatives to meet these problems. Often the deep-seated reasons are to do with discovering one's personality and a meaning to life, in which case we can share our Christian faith in well-reasoned and relevant ways.

Real drug addiction is very much more serious and needs specialist treatment and advice. Addicts need to be desperate for help before you can get very much further than general friendship, and even then they need permanent residential treatment and very thorough rehabilitation and after-care, preferably at a Christian centre. Many experienced Christian workers see drug addiction as a particularly violent assault by the powers of evil to establish a hold on human lives.[1] Certainly it is clear that without a spiritual deliverance through Jesus Christ it is very rare indeed for an addict to be cured.

Our attitude as Christians must therefore be one of genuine concern and compassion. We know that man is not merely a chemical apparatus, but a living soul, made in God's image and responsible to him. One of the great New Testament principles is that the Christian belongs to one Master and in God's power resists anything else that would rule over him. 'As a Christian I *may* do anything, but that does not mean that everything is good for me. I may do everything, but I must not be the slave of anything,' wrote Paul (1 Cor. 6:12, J. B. Phillips). Anything which impedes my self-control, as drug-taking certainly does (and aims to do) and as alcohol does, is dishonouring the body God has given me and makes a mockery both of

[1] See Tomkinson, Bird and Ramsey, *Christianity and Addictions* (New Life Press).

my Christian commitment and of the work of Christ to redeem me. It is always a primary method of the devil's attacks to try to knock out the rational in man, to by-pass and eventually destroy the mind.

Should a Christian then inform the college authorities when he knows that drugs are being peddled and used? This is a vexed question to which there is no glib answer. If we do this, should we also report sexual offences, stealing, cheating in exams, *etc.*? Clearly we are not to be self-appointed moral policemen. Also, the people concerned are known to us; they may be friends or friends of friends, and we do not want to see them thrown out and their whole future career jeopardized. Yet a powerful argument in the other direction is that it may well be in the student's best long-term interest. The path to addiction may be barred by action at an early stage, and discovery by the college authorities then may well be less calamitous than discovery by the police later. This may in fact be the best, or only, way to rescue the situation. But we should not report individuals unless we have talked to them personally and taken every opportunity to reason things out with them. We must be able to tell them about it and the reasons why we intend to take action. If someone is known to be a 'pusher', however, then we should not hesitate to expose this as it may prevent many from being caught in his net. He may be an addict in need of help and we can never ignore the needs of the person, but this may also provide a link to the source of the drugs and help to stem the tide of corruption. Each of us will have to decide according to the circumstances of the individual case, but we must not decide on a basis of sentiment, so much as with a sense of responsibility to the whole of society and a determination to overcome evil with good.

Spiritism

Another area in which a good deal of interest has been aroused among students in recent years is that of spiritism and the occult. It holds a fatal fascination for fallen man. Spiritist séances are held in many halls of residence and many individuals have experimented with ouija boards and other means of contacting the spirit world. It often begins as a 'game' for dabblers, but it quickly exercises a malign influence and magnetism over those who 'experiment' because it seems to offer knowledge of the spiritual realm and experience of spiritual power quite independently of God.

The Bible contains many warnings against it in both Old and New Testaments. 'Do not turn to mediums or wizards; do not seek them out, to be defiled by them: I am the Lord your God' (Lv. 19:31). '(Manasseh) . . . practised soothsaying and augury, and dealt with mediums and with wizards. He did much evil in the sight of the Lord, provoking him to anger' (2 Ki. 21:6). Even more clear is Isaiah 8:19, 20: 'And when they say to you, "Consult the mediums and the wizards who chirp and mutter," should not a people consult their God? Should they consult the dead on behalf of the living? To the teaching and to the testimony!'

The New Testament clearly links the work of evil spirits and the practice of magic and divination. Passages in Acts 13, 16 and 19 all show how these things are bound together, with disastrous results to those who become enmeshed by them.

We should never underestimate the power of the devil or treat lightly such manifestations of evil. Some may be psychological in origin, but there are very real forces of evil at work in many cases. We need to be aware of the clear biblical prohibitions in this realm and avoid any undue inquisitiveness. For example, it is never wise to go to a séance with the purpose merely of finding out what is going on. It is better for a group of Christians to get together to pray, when they know a séance is going to take place, in a room quite separate from its location, binding the work of evil in the name of Jesus. The effect has often been to pray the séance out of existence. On the other hand we are not to become obsessed with the problem and see more of the devil at every hand than we do of the Lord. We need to be humble, recognizing that we have no strength of our own with which to fight the devil, but we must also be fearless, for in Christ there is always victory.

> 'Jesus is stronger than Satan or sin;
> Satan to Jesus must bow.'

So while the forces opposing us are real and active, they are also defeated — and they know it. We must not allow our energies to be diverted on to this front. There are far bigger battles to be fought for the salvation of sinners and the upbuilding of Christians. We shall not therefore be going out of our way for an encounter with evil, face to face, but if we are forced to fight we need to use the whole armour of God and to be sure that we are fully equipped and prepared at any moment. Never deal with these problems alone. Always work as a group of praying Christians, claiming the protection of the blood of Christ. Involve older and more experienced Christians who have had previous experience of work in this realm. Anyone who has been actively involved should be urged to repent and destroy all links with evil practices. There must be a clear break and the cleansing of the blood of Jesus for the grip of evil to be broken.

You may discover that people have come under bad influences by means of meditation techniques, yoga, or some Oriental religion such as the currently popular Divine Light Mission. Many of these influences seem to be tied up with idolatry and even demonic agencies. Here again the initial attraction has often been the promise of discovering a meaning and purpose in life.

Guru Maharaj Ji claims to offer 'divine light' and 'knowledge', which is said to lift one out of the sense levels of everyday existence into the inner harmony of pure consciousness. There is often a tangible physical experience of a blinding light which followers of the guru undoubtedly have, but which seems to leave the devotee less capable of thinking rationally and less able to cope with life than before. This seems to be a spiritual experience, but its origin is clearly not of God. The subtlety of this strange movement is that its followers are at pains to make it appear compatible with Christianity. Their meetings often include Christian songs with subtle changes of the words, or are punctuated by shouts of 'Praise the Lord'. They would allow Jesus the title of Perfect Master for his own time, but the guru is the reincarnation of Jesus and he is today's spiritual master. So he is worshipped and obeyed. It is another manifestation of the fact that man is incurably religious. He is made for God and can find no true rest or significance apart from him.

In this chapter we have ranged over a wide and representative area of interests and involvements which the Christian is likely to encounter in his own relationships as a student. The false trails that are followed, and the disillusionment that inevitably results, point to the inescapable fact that horizontal relationships between men can find their true perspective only when the individual's vertical relationship with the living God has been restored, through Christ. I can know myself truly and live in harmony both with myself and with my fellow-men only when I know God as my personal Heavenly Father, recognize that I am accepted by him and seek to love him with my whole being. This is a Christian student's unique contribution in the field of relationships in the student world. Because he knows his God, he has come to discover his true self and is set free in that discovery to love and serve both God and his fellow-men.

6 Thinking things through

Christians in their right spiritual senses have always realized that they live on this earth in space and time, as citizens of another kingdom that is eternal. In one sense this world is our home, because it is our Father's creation and everything that happens to it and to us is subject to his sovereign rule. He created it good, as a place for man to dwell in and to develop, and he sustains and governs its progress. He is 'upholding the universe by his word of power' (Heb. 1:3). Yet in another sense it is in rebel hands and under an alien government. Fallen man gives his allegiance to the prince of this world, and although the devil is only a creature of God and cannot lift a finger beyond what God's sovereignty allows, yet it is true that mankind is held captive by him so that 'the whole world is in the power of the evil one' (1 Jn. 5:19).

As Christians we live in the tension between these two basic facts. Sometimes the enmity of the world against God's people has been, and is, undisguised and quite open. They are brought before kings and governors, hunted in dens and caves of the earth, imprisoned, tortured, killed, for the sake of Christ. At other times it is considerably more subtle, almost undetectable, and probably even more dangerous. One of the greatest weapons used against the Christian church in the Western world today is the hostility of apathy. When Jesus warned his followers about wolves in sheep's clothing (Mt. 7:15), he was showing that some of the most devastating attacks the church would have to face would be unheralded and disguised. The wolf does not announce his presence.

In terms of our life as Christians at college, therefore, it is important that we recognize this backcloth to what we are doing. We need to bring a distinctly Christian perspective to our work and involvement, and to be realistic about the climate in which we are called to live, so that the Christian witness in our colleges will not just exist, but grow stronger and deeper.

In all this the crucial area is the Christian's mind. This is where the attacks of evil always centre because it is the central citadel of human personality, where words and actions find their origin. God has ordained the mind to be the primary medium through which he communicates with man, and man with God. It is by the communication to the mind of man of the truth of who God is and what he has done in Christ that the new birth begins. That is why Paul's concern in his evangelism was with the content of the message — the objective, historical facts of God's intervention in the life, death and resurrection of Jesus Christ. It is by 'the renewal of your mind' that the Christian is transformed and proves the will of God to be perfect (Rom. 12:2). Christian truth challenges the will through the mind, and this must never be short-circuited. Part of our being made in the image of God is the fact that we have the ability to think and so to choose. Indeed, all our actions are to be governed by our thought; the mind is the control-centre of our behaviour. For example, when Paul is dealing with the problem of immorality in the church at Corinth (an emotional area of behaviour, it might be argued) his approach is entirely to the mind. He reasons with them from basic Christian principles and concludes, 'Do you not know that your body is a temple of the Holy Spirit within you, which you have from God?' (1 Cor. 6:19). What we know with our minds governs how we act in our bodies. And this principle holds good in a thousand-and-one reflex actions and off-the-cuff remarks throughout every day of our lives.[1]

[1] See also John R. W. Stott's booklet *Your Mind Matters* (IVP).

It is hardly surprising, then, that the devil's attacks, not least in student life, should centre on the Christian's mind, for he is well aware that to knock out that centre is to win the day. Today's battle is still for men's minds and if we are going to do more than merely survive as Christians at college, if we are going to become more like Christ and serve him better, then we need to devote our attention to this most vital and significant area of the conflict.

In his book *The Image*,[2] Professor Daniel Boorstin quotes the following conversation:

> 'ADMIRING FRIEND: My, that's a beautiful baby you have there!
>
> MOTHER: Oh, that's nothing — you should see his photograph.'

Boorstin's penetrating analysis of modern society develops the thesis that we have come to value the illusion more than reality, that life is lived second-hand and we are no longer able to determine what is real. Much of the conditioning of our society predisposes us towards a view of life which makes our goal both having our cake and eating it — to look younger as we grow older, to exploit the world's resources without exhausting them, to work less for more money, to get a 'first' without working at all. It is all an illusion; life is not like that and yet we are all aware of living in this sort of pressurized dream society. What was a drift away from reality and even rationality ten years ago is now beginning to assume the proportions of a tidal wave. There is very strong pressure on us to retreat from the rational into our own illusions.

As Christians we ought not to be surprised or caught off guard by these currents in contemporary society, especially student society. We recognize that there is a strong tide away from thinking and towards feeling as the ground of action. Evidence of this is not hard to find.

[2] Daniel J. Boorstin, *The Image, or What Happened to the American Dream* (Penguin Books).

Many students find their enjoyment in letting their minds blow, losing themselves in the disco, or the cinema, or in Tolkien — any 'unreal' world will do. Some would even go so far as to say that what significance they have found in life they have found there — one step away from reality. Others, more politically orientated, may advocate a violent revolution or even anarchy as the only possible answer to the mess that Rationality has got us into. Break it all down and start again — at least it can't possibly be as bad as the present set-up. And there will be times when the Christian finds that he has some sympathy with that sort of feeling, because Rationalism (man's mind-power used without reference to God) has got us into a mess. His answer is totally different, however, since he knows that anti-Rationalism is equally godless and a road to even greater chaos. Still others see the only way out in terms of a journey backwards in time, back to nature and the primitive, the total rejection of science and its technology.

You can multiply examples, but the point is that the Christian's mind is not immune from this kind of moulding simply because he is a Christian. The battle is on and he is in the thick of it. Sometimes the pressures will exhibit themselves in particular forms of 'Christianized' unreality. Many of our church services, or activities in the Christian Union, can take place in an atmosphere of super-spirituality which is far removed from the everyday world in which God has put us. In some Christian groups this appears in the way that 'feeling led' becomes an automatic justification of any particular course of action. This is at best subjective and prone to all sorts of personal quirks, and at worst degenerates into a form of blackmail where those with the strongest feelings, often the most dominant personalities, exert their own control over the whole group. Isn't 'thinking led' really the more biblical way of doing things? Of course we can swing to the opposite extreme and become rigidly intellectual — all head and no heart — which is equally unbalanced, but in most cases that seems a much rarer danger at the present time.

The Christian's resources

The Christian faces the pressures common to all his contemporaries, but, unlike them, he has unique resources with which to meet them. He has a true perspective on reality because he is beginning to learn to see things from God's viewpoint, through the Scriptures, and by means of the Holy Spirit's work within him. He has entered into a spiritual reality which opens up a whole new world of experience in Christ. The Holy Spirit living in him, the Spirit of power, love and self-control (2 Tim. 1:7), not only enables him to make a right (a real) analysis of himself and his situations with his renewed mind, but also energizes him to take the appropriate action, in trust and obedience. Mind and heart, truth and experience thus become forged together in a new life and outlook. We must at all costs avoid an unbiblical separation between mind and spirit, as though one were evil and the other good, or as though the emotions were less fallen and somehow more trustworthy than the mind. So many of our problems in living the Christian life are due to the fact that we listen far more to our feelings than to what we know is true because it is taught by God's Word. The same tendency is present in the kind of evangelism in which Jesus is portrayed as the latest in mind-blowing experience — only this one is eternal, the ultimate. All this is sub-Christian. We must have a fully biblical view of what it means to be a whole man, and of Christ meeting every facet and area of our life with his completeness. And from this will come a coherent world-view on which to build. It will take time, of course, yet here is the Christian's greatest potential strength and present weakness in today's society.

The trouble is that many of us, as Christians, are woefully ignorant of the Bible. We have our proof-texts up our sleeves ready for witnessing, but we have not really begun to think biblically about our life in the student community or our involvement in society at large. John Bunyan was said to have 'bibline' blood: the Bible was his source of life and circulated to every part of his being. Every Christian should belong to that blood group! When we start to operate the Bible's principles of action seriously in every area of our lives, then we shall begin to make a more distinctively Christian impact on our society.

The Bible is not a book of restrictive rules, or of neatly sewn-up arguments; it leaves a great deal of the application and thinking to us. But it is a book of God-given and binding principles. This is God's view of reality. The Bible's picture is of the world as it really is, so that to try to live in it without reference to God's principles is to fly in the face of reality. Although man may imagine that he can safely ignore the natural and spiritual laws of God's world, since God has constructed reality, in fact he never can. A broken (or ignored) law in the end breaks man. Law-breaking has within it the seeds of self-destruction. The law of gravity provides an obvious example in the physical realm. You cannot afford to ignore or flout it.

The same principle holds good in man's encounter with God's reality in every other area and at every level of experience. So, in basic terms, the Ten Commandments are not arbitrary restrictions on a primitive nomadic people, or even a record of their social conventions. They are binding principles for man, at any point of time or space, because they are related to the way man is made, and to break them is to fight against reality as God has created it. The man who tries to work a seven-day week will suffer, physically and probably psychologically. A society in which theft and dishonesty are tolerated is sowing the seeds of its own decline and eventual collapse. When sexual intercourse is not confined to marriage, not only do the individuals concerned debase their own bodies, but society is weakened by ignoring the God-given structure of life-long marriage and the family. All sorts of jealousies and insecurities follow in its wake, not least the severe damage often done to the innocent children unhappily brought up in such an environment. These are absolute principles and the man who lives against them is working for the destruction of his own humanity and the breakdown of his society. All these are basic examples of the pervading principle that we must apply the clear teaching of the Bible to the whole spectrum of our involvement in the world.

A further example would be one of the great intellectual debates of this decade on the nature of man. Is he merely a naked ape, a programmed machine, a chemical reaction, meaningless dust? So many of the problems encountered by Christian students in their academic work, which attack their faith and cause panic, can be traced to this basic issue. The Christian has in the Bible the Creator's view. That does not mean that neat, pre-packed answers to all our intellectual questions are available. There are some things which are beyond the finite mind of man to comprehend anyway, and others which God has chosen not to disclose, but we do have authoritative teaching on all the basic principles we need. God gives us the tools with which to build, but we have to do the work. We have the 'pattern of sound words', the architect's plan, which determines the building's construction.

In what ways is man unique, being made 'in the image of God', and in what senses is he an animal? What effect has the fall of Adam had upon that image? How should God's mandate to man to 'have dominion' be exercised today? What is the value of the tiny speck of dust called man within a vast universe of infinite complexity? These are the questions we must be asking, recognizing that we do have a base to work from, which is true because it is revealed by the God who is Truth, and which is unchanging because it is grounded in his eternal character. It is not humility to pretend otherwise, but faithlessness.

It goes without saying, then, that the Christian student should be as fully involved in the life of his college or university as possible. There is no room for the sort of monasticism which, sadly, has characterized some Christians in the past. They are either working, attending Christian meetings, or eating at the 'Christian table' in hall. We are never taught by the Bible to form a Christian ghetto. Its emphasis is rather on Christian penetration of the whole of society — the salt preserving the meat from corruption, the light scattering the darkness.

One of the reasons why contemporary Christians are less effectively involved in the world than our predecessors have often been seems to be that we have cocooned ourselves within an evangelical life-style, which virtually precludes any close contacts or friendships with non-Christians. It would be easy for the same pattern to develop in student life, especially for those who have come up from a traditional church background, but it must be firmly resisted. This stems partly from a false dichotomy in our thinking between the spiritual and the secular.

Sometimes Christians have been trapped into thinking that evangelism, prayer and Bible study are the only things that really matter, and that unless you are engaged in these things you are not serving God at all. But the whole of life belongs to God, as does the whole of our beings and personalities. All our gifts and abilities can be used for his service and every aspect of our lives should be lived for him. We serve him not just in our 'religious' activities, but every hour of the day — or else we serve ourselves. Nor does this mean that the normal Christian never talks of anything but specifically Christian things, or spends all the time he is not actually working in specifically evangelistic activity. That may be God's calling to a few, but it is not the norm. We are not all made (or re-made!) that way and we should not become a prey to guilt feelings if we are not. Christian maturity is measured in terms of likeness to the Lord Jesus Christ in character, not by activity.

God's plan involves different members of the Christian body being involved in as many areas of student life as time and their natural talents will allow. Indeed, the more areas in which Christians can be actively demonstrating the reality of their beliefs the better. It is right and worth while, in itself, for a Christian to join the choral society or the soccer club, or whatever else he enjoys doing, simply because he enjoys it and wants to use and develop his God-given talents in that way, or to discover new ones. He does not need the justification of 'making contacts'; that is to misread God's world and the purposes behind his creation. Living a normal life, as a consistent Christian, will inevitably make its mark and in itself be the sort of natural witness which God can and will use.

Life at college provides some marvellous opportunities to widen our horizons and branch out into new areas of interest and involvement. A Christian should never be a bore — Jesus wasn't. But sadly many of his followers have become narrow in the wrong sense and eliminated all their points of contact with the world. At this stage of life God's calling for you is to be a student, so enter into it whole-heartedly and live as full a student life as you can. It is by this that you will glorify God in doing his will.

There is, of course, a right sense in which the Christian's life is narrow — with regard to evil. There is a restriction on sin, which we recognize as the other face of our freedom. To shun evil is not cowardice, but common sense. Most of our practical difficulties, however, come in what might be called the 'grey' areas of life and behaviour, where there is no clear direction from Scripture and where it is hard to use categories of right and wrong. Opinion will differ among Christians, often between the generations. The problem may well be to sort out what is binding because it is a biblical principle, and what is a social convention from a past age, a tradition of the forefathers.

Making decisions about matters of this sort is part of a Christian's development to maturity and so we should not shrink from thinking and praying them through, and standing by what we believe to be right. We need to employ all the resources God has given us, under the supreme authority of his Word. We need also to recognize that equally sincere Christians may come to quite opposite conclusions in matters of this sort, on which they will agree to differ. We must not allow conflicting views over less than basic issues to divide Christians who are otherwise united in Christ by the gospel. We must preserve our unity in the things that matter most. It is important also to preserve our liberty in Christ (Gal. 5:1) and not to allow our Christian life to be reduced to a matter of keeping man-made rules. Each of us is accountable to God for our own actions.

One of the basic biblical principles is therefore that we are not to be condemnatory of others. Paul expands this in some detail in Romans 14:1-4 and 10-13. The positive action here is never to put a hindrance in the way of a brother. We are to look to ourselves and see that we are right before God. Again, we are given some searching criteria for evaluating our involvement in the world in 1 Corinthians 6:12 and 10:23. There are three penetrating questions to ask, if we have decided that something is 'lawful', or permitted. (1) Is it helpful to my Christian life? That is, is it advantageous or profitable for me? (2) Is it tending to enslave me? Does it rule over me and start to call the tune? (3) Does it build me up? In other words, the thrust of our examination should be not 'What's wrong with doing it?' so much as asking what positive good will come of it.

In addition to these personal considerations the New Testament impresses upon us a concern for the unhindered growth of our fellow-Christians (Rom. 15:1, 2) and our supreme motivation that we should please and honour the Lord (1 Pet. 2:9). Every Christian has his Bible and his knees with which to work out these things in detail for himself. We must be concerned to be both biblical *and* twentieth-century Christians.

We may find that our involvement brings us into an environment which is quite inimical to Christianity, but if we are there because God has taken us there, we can rely on him to keep us and use us. For example, one Christian who was a member of his hockey club exercised a great influence for good. He went to the annual dinner, enjoyed himself very much but refused to get drunk. Consequently, at the end of the evening he was the only person able to take the two most incapable members back to their hall and put them to bed. Later on he was able to tell them why, and his unobtrusive Christianity set many of his colleagues thinking. Another example comes to mind of a Christian student who became editor of his university newspaper. At the time it was almost bankrupt and on the verge of ceasing publication, since the previous terms' issues had been so obscene that most of the local tradesmen had withdrawn their advertising, which had been the main financial support, rather than be associated with it. Starting from rock bottom, he was able to build up both the readership and local confidence, making the magazine economically viable again by the sheer weight of positive, interesting content. Christian involvement will not necessarily have such a clear 'pay-off' of course, but our presence, as long as we are salty and 'savourful', will affect our surroundings.

Student politics

It is good to know that an increasing number of Christians are becoming actively involved in student politics and being elected to office within the Students Unions. There are also faculty or department committees in almost all universities and some colleges, on which there is considerable student representation, and management committees in almost all halls of residence. You may well discover that this sort of involvement is part of your call as a Christian, through personal inclination and interest, or perhaps through pressure of circumstances.

At present most of the Student Unions are dominated almost entirely by a vocal Leftist minority, owing to the virtual abdication of its voting rights by the silent, apathetic majority. The Left is itself often split between different warring sects and appears to be more concerned about internecine strife than a stable and equitable structure of life in the student community. The outcome is that there is something of a vacuum in student politics which presents an opportunity for Christians to be involved, on specifically Christian principles, such as the value and significance of the individual, honesty and integrity, equality of opportunity.

Most students want a stable and just society in which to live and work, but vocal propaganda does have an effect. As Christians, we shall have to use our minds to formulate cogent reasons for our action in a particular situation, but if it is based on a true (that is, biblical) understanding of man, it may well command much more general support than we would think. This has happened on several occasions when Christians have thought it right to rally to a cause, such as opposition to the installation of a contraceptive-vending machine, or to the innovation of mixed washing arrangements in a hall. They have received considerable support from the 'moderate' majority and won the day. We cannot expect to impose Christian standards on a non-Christian community, but we are to stem the tide of evil wherever we can, and should certainly represent and urge our own views because we believe them to be for the greatest good.

A further distinctive mark of Christian concern, and the cause of most of the difficulties Christian students face when they do get involved, is that their contribution is not on doctrinaire, conventional party lines. Christians are to be found on both sides of the political argument, as should be expected. The Christian student may find it very hard to be a party man in the present climate. At times you may find yourself campaigning for a reform of which the Establishment seems wilfully ignorant, or to which it is deliberately opposed. At other times you may find yourself standing with the administration.

Except for the extremes, party lines in student politics are not very strong, but you must be prepared for some tension when your principles are deeper and broader than a party line and when you may not sink your conscience for a party. It may hurt; but consistent Christian integrity does win respect. You will need a tough skin and a strong faith. Take, for example, your attitude to a protest demonstration, a sit-in, or a rent strike, or to the question of whether it is ever permissible to use violence. Issues like these demand not only a careful, detailed study of all the circumstances of a given situation, but a firm grasp of biblical principles (*e.g.* Rom. 13:1-7) and a determination to see these enacted as far as possible. There is plenty of material for study in Paul's attitude to secular authorities in the Acts, as well as the minor prophets such as Amos, and the book of Revelation.

None of this, of course, means that the Christian is automatically the answer to society's problems! He needs continually to be aware of the implications of his actions on the lives of others, and to relate them to Christ's principles. Perhaps worst of all would be to rally a Christian lobby to elect Christians to office, however unsuited they might be, just on the grounds that they are Christians. But an increasing number of Christians do find themselves in positions where they have great potential for good. Very often real causes of grievance have been overlooked because a small coterie of 'popular' people have been in power. Here the Christian can bring about genuine reforms and sometimes help to retrieve moral and social situations which would otherwise degenerate, to the detriment of everybody in the community.

Involvement in any of these ways will make demands upon our time and energies. Our life in this world is to be seen in the context of a spiritual warfare, in which every Christian is inevitably involved. Sometimes the opposition is from outside, from other people, though we must then recognize that we are 'not contending against flesh and blood, but against principalities, against the powers, against the world rulers of this present darkness, against the spiritual hosts of wickedness in the heavenly places' (Eph. 6:12). But equally often the pressure arises within ourselves. It's probably true that every Christian student who becomes seriously involved in thinking through his academic work, or in relating his faith to the problems of society, will sooner or later be beset by doubts and seemingly insoluble problems. We all know of apparently committed Christians who seem to lose their faith while they are at college, and in one sense the new student is right to be alarmed at such a prospect. The answer, however, is emphatically *not* to refuse to think. This only means that your faith is as immature and weak at the end as it was at the beginning, which is not really a serious option.

One of the main reasons why students 'lose their faith' is that it was never really a faith of their own at all. They were carried along in the wake of other keen Christians, perhaps in a youth fellowship or Bible study class, without ever coming to a personal repentance and faith in Christ. Many, of course, discover this in their first few weeks at college and do become Christians in a personal sense, but others get blown right off course. It is a very useful exercise for the new student from a Christian background to make sure that he knows what he believes and has some reasons for his faith before he goes to college, and more important still that he asks, 'Is *my* trust in Christ? Is my life beginning to be regulated by him?' We are all of us learning and working out our faith in the process of everyday living, and there can be no substitute for that. But if the new student finds himself in real perplexity, then it is well worth talking things over with an older Christian, his minister or youth leader, before actually leaving the home environment. Real faith is never static but always growing, and one of the key development points will be the first few days at college. It is very important not to be ashamed of being known as a Christian from the start, to keep your eyes open for other Christians and to join up with them in fellowship. Don't worry about what your initial impression of them may be, or of what they think about you. You belong together, because you belong to the Lord.

But, however committed we may be, most of us go through a deep examination of aspects of our faith while at college. There is nothing unusual or wrong about this, although sometimes the going can seem very tough indeed. One of the important things to do in a situation like that is to look our doubts in the face and examine them and their origins critically. Sometimes the doubts we experience are due to the fact that our personal relationship with God has been blunted, or even severed temporarily, by sin. God seems distant, even unreal; the Bible holds no interest or attraction for us; prayer is an empty duty. Here the problem may well be moral and spiritual, and that can be very hard to admit. It's more satisfying to intellectualize it. But no amount of searching for new light will save the situation if we are sinning against the light we have and deliberately disobeying God.

In dealing with doubts and temptations it is usually a help to realize that I am not alone in the history of Christianity in facing this problem. And today, even in my circle of friends, others are having similar experiences. A sense of isolation is one of the most numbing effects of our doubts and problems. So do be prepared to share the difficulty with other Christians. Too often we imagine that they will think us silly or heretical, but it is surprising how often in discussion we discover that others have faced the same problem and been helped to work it through.

Before sharing with others, if you are reticent, it can be a help to get things down on paper and see just how big (or small) the issue really is. Imaginary consequences of unproven possibilities have an alarming way of dominating a situation and immersing us in unnecessary despair. It can be a comfort to realize that just because you have not yet found an answer to the problem it does not mean that one does not exist. You may find that Christian books help. Above all, go on thinking and bringing your problem to God. He alone is the source of all true enlightenment, but so often we go on puzzling things out, a bit stubbornly, without calling for light. It may be that your problem is one to which there is no glib solution. Perhaps it has perplexed the best minds of the church down the centuries. On the one hand we need the humility that does not dismiss the Christian faith just because there are depths of paradox within it that defy the neat solutions of our finite minds. On the other, we need courage to go on nibbling at the problem, conscious that our contribution can only be infinitesimally small, but aware of the value of that, if it helps us to understand the truth of God more fully.

There should be in the fellowship of every Christian Union a loving, uncritical sounding-board for our most persistent doubts and 'heresies'. We need one another to keep ourselves within the biblical faith. The sort of fellowship which carries an invisible banner, 'We have no problems here', is untrue to itself and to its Lord. We all have problems, but we know where to take them and how to begin dealing with them. To do this within a real fellowship can be one of the most stimulating and strengthening experiences of our Christian lives. Our concern for truth and our desire to be biblical Christians must never be allowed to shape us into the sort of people whom Tennyson described as 'icily regular, faultily faultless and splendidly null'. It is only as we learn to love and serve one another within God's family that the reality of the gospel is demonstrated to the world around.

So there is a war on, and we, as Christians, are to be fully involved. We realize that the history of the world in which we are caught up is neither shapeless nor without purpose. The climax to which we are all moving is the demonstration to all of Jesus Christ as Lord, when he comes to wind up history and reign eternally. We have the privilege of getting on with it until he comes. On the personal level, this means living today in the light of that day as a faithful steward of all that I have been given, aware of my accountability to God, but aware also of his immense resources at my disposal. Student life, seen in this context, is a short episode in our preparation for life and eternity. Brief; but crucial. For example, we shall not have opportunities to study like this again. Our fellow-students are more open now to the gospel than they are likely to be again. We have more time and opportunities to be involved as a Christian in a host of different activities. But we are also laying foundations for a lifetime of service for Christ. We want to see Christians grow in their personal faith, and increase in numbers as they expand their influence into every area of student society. But beyond that we want to see a growing flood of students leaving college or university to go out into all the professions, throughout the world, to serve the Lord until he returns. We want to see the effect of this in court rooms and hospitals, classrooms and mission stations, boardrooms and pulpits, at kitchen sinks and on the shop floor, because Christians genuinely live out in these situations the faith they profess. We want to see this nation's life turned back to God because his Spirit has equipped a living, growing army of Christians who mean business in his power. We want to see this happening throughout the global village, as Christ's kingdom grows.

Isn't it worth giving your student days unreservedly to Christ for that end? Can we do anything other than love and serve him to our utmost limit, with all we have and are?